THE SECRETS OF
BRITAIN

Andy Williams (England and Wales photographs) studied photography at Guildford School of Art. He is acknowledged to be one of Britain's foremost landscape photographers, and pictures from his library have appeared in books, brochures, calendars, greetings cards and posters all over the world. He uses a 5 x 4 inch camera with lenses from 65 mm to 500 mm for his landscape and architecture photography, but also has a 6 x 7 cm outfit for, as he puts it, 'anything that moves'. He is totally dedicated to his profession and strives to produce beautiful images of the world about us, concentrating his skills mainly in the United Kingdom, where nothing gives him greater pleasure than to record on film the ever-changing moods of nature. So if you come across a small man waiting patiently beside a large camera atop a tripod, you will know it is 'the happiest man he knows'!

Dennis Hardley (Scotland photographs) was born in Blitz-sieged Liverpool in 1940, where he spent his teenage years doing odd jobs for the Beatles before becoming a Concorde engineer. Dennis first became a photographer as an RAF civilian in 1972, supplying pictures to *Scots Magazine*. In 1973 he moved to Scotland with his family and established himself as a professional photographer. He has since driven over a million miles in his pursuit of photographing the Scottish landscape, and this is the sixth book to feature his work.

Tamsin Pickeral (text) graduated from Reading University with an honours degree in History of Art and Architecture. Following further studying in Italy, the author turned her attentions to adventure. She has travelled extensively, and has recently returned to Britain having spent the last nine years living on a cattle ranch in the US. Prior to that she lived in Italy, and has journeyed through most of Europe and across Australia. Despite her wanderlust it is Britain that she keeps returning to, finding it an endless source of inspiration for her books. When not exploring the British countryside, the author divides her time between her beloved horses and writing.

This is a **STAR FIRE** Book

STAR FIRE BOOKS
Crabtree Hall
Crabtree Lane
Fulham
London SW6 6TY
www.flametreepublishing.com

Star Fire is part of The Foundry Creative Media Company Limited

Copyright © 2005 The Foundry

All Photography by Andy Williams except
Scotland photographs by Dennis Hardley www.scotphoto.com

05 07 09 08 06
1 3 5 7 9 10 8 6 4 2

ISBN 1 84451 301 7

Printed in China

Thanks to: Frances Bodiam, Chris Herbert, Julia Rolf, Mike Spender, Claire Walker and Polly Willis

THE SECRETS OF
BRITAIN

PHOTOGRAPHS BY ANDY WILLIAMS & DENNIS HARDLEY

Text by Tamsin Pickeral

STAR
FIRE

Contents

Introduction

THE PACE OF LIFE BEATS FAST IN TODAY'S SOCIETY; UNWITTINGLY THE MAJORITY FINDS ITSELF LOCKED IN THE GREATER MECHANISMS, THE VAST, ENDLESSLY TURNING WHEELS OF BIG BUSINESS AND TIGHT SCHEDULES, JUGGLING TOO MANY THINGS WITH TOO FEW HANDS.

To take hold of the corporate heart and kill the insistent pulse of stress is to shake loose, throw off the bonds of restriction and step into a world of glorious scenery; a hidden treasure trove of inspirational landscape, the history of its past, and the eminence of the nation – this is the world of *The Secrets of Britain*. This wonderful collection of photographs of some of the famous and not so famous corners of Britain offers a glimpse at the sedate, the quiet, and the idyllic, a respite from the loud cacophony of everyday life. Here Britain of both the past and present is captured by the keen eye of the photographic artist in a series of evocative shots.

Overwhelmingly, Britain is a country of diversity, but the threads of difference are unilaterally knotted in the one single fact of its island status. Surrounded by water, Britain's character and history have been shaped in great part by this phenomenon.

The combined masses of England, Scotland and Wales form the largest island in Europe, with a stunningly varied coastline some 6,000 miles (9,655 km) long. The difference between the smooth serene Bay of Glenuig, Moidart, off the west coast of Scotland, and the rugged beauty of Bedruthan Steps at the opposite end of the country in Cornwall, is as poignant as the cultural divide between the two places. The great white cliffs of Dover on the south-east coast – synonymous with England and long the romantic subject of artists, poets and writers – gleam against the sea, a stalwart barricade looking towards the coast of France some

21 miles (34 km) away. In East Anglia the flat landscape struggles against the battering North Sea, much of the country lying below sea level and formed from reclaimed land. The salt marshes, eerie carpets of sodden ground and resilient rushes, sway to the piping song of the oystercatcher and hide rare nesting birds. Here great towns have disappeared beneath the relentless sea; Dunwich, once a thriving port and the seat of the first East Anglican Christian Bishop in the sixth century, was swallowed by the waves; the ruins of churches are now a playground for fish. On the west coast the great Cambrian Mountains of Wales tumble into Cardigan Bay and the Bristol Channel; the Stack Rocks at St Govan's Head, Pembrokeshire, scatter into the sea, watched over by the tiny one-room chapel to St Govan, clinging to the steep, rocky cliff edge. Further up the west coast, leaving Wales behind, one stumbles upon Blackpool, kitsch and exciting; the tower a beacon welcoming holidaymakers from miles around.

Each and every county has its own identity, dialect, expressions and character. Scotland and Wales are separate again; fiercely patriotic and nationalistic, they retain their own signature, won through long years of battle and blood. Wales is a small country with a huge, brave heart. The Cambrian Mountains form the backbone of Wales, running from the great Mount Snowdon in the north to the Brecon Beacons in the south. This is the place of myths and strange tales, Welsh folklore, stories of saints and heroes, ghosts and unexplained events; the beauty of the landscape, mountains and lakes inspires even the dullest imagination.

From mountains and lakes to mountains and lochs, and so to Scotland. The Cheviot Hills of Northumberland roll into the Scottish Lowlands. Northumberland and

Scotland have suffered an uneasy marriage in past years; Northumberland caught in the border wars, a frontier county between the Scots and English. Cross the border into Scotland and you enter a new realm. To enter Scotland is to tread into a land of untamed beauty. Wild countryside, expanses of hills and mountains with little human population. This is the landscape that inspired a host of writers and painters, Sir Walter Scott, Robert Burns, Allan Ramsay and Sir Henry Raeburn to name just a few. Across Scotland crumbling castles defiantly brace the elements, vestiges of the days of fortifications, battles and wagers – not just between the Scottish and English, but between the Lowlanders and the Highlanders, too. To the east sits Edinburgh, to the west Glasgow; two cities of elegance and refinement, bastions to the art and literary worlds, home to great architecture old and new. Further north still and into the Highlands. Lonely, desolate and utterly lovely, the Highlands and Islands of Scotland make up one quarter of Britain's land mass. Not all is natural wilderness; the 'fair city' of Perth is the cosmopolitan jewel of Scotland's north-east coast line. This ancient city was once the capital of Scotland until James I was murdered there in 1437 and his family escaped south to Edinburgh.

To the south lies northern England, the industrial heart of the country; scarred through the rise of the industrial revolution, the coal to a fire of progress. Still amongst the debris of an unplanned pregnancy of economy, a fruitful end to a painful labour, northern England retains much of its original beauty – it is easy to look beyond the aesthetic blight of industrialism and see the treasure beneath. The coal mines

of Sheffield, the ship-building along the banks of the River Tyne, and the iron works – all this, and yet this region is also home to the beautiful Yorkshire Dales and the scenic Pennines, Britain's spine of hills running from Derbyshire to Northumberland. The Yorkshire area bears industry as a necessary evil, but the town of York, with her inspiring York Minster, wipes it clean. Newcastle-upon-Tyne is a northern captain of industry but also one of the best examples of Victorian town planning; she now welcomes the weary traveller with the stunning image of a bronze angel, set high on a hill above Tyneside.

From one extreme to another, Tyneside to England's boot – Cornwall, Devon and Somerset – the south-west counties are a world apart. Here the climate is warmer, the terrain open moors, forests and rolling hills. The coastline is ragged, picturesque, beaten by the Atlantic, moulded, shaped and eaten away to great chunks of jagged rocks; surprising bays of sandy beaches are tucked amongst the granite headlands. Part of the irrepressible appeal of Britain is her past, both historical and mythical; the boot of Britain poking into the Atlantic is shrouded in the tales of King Arthur, stories that whisper up the coastline and into Wales. The land is thick with Arthurian reference, from the site of Tintagel where King Arthur had his castle, to St Michael's Mount, part of the legendary lost kingdom of Lyonesse, where Arthur's knights once rode. Other legends abound too: there is the beast of Bodmin Moor, the ghosts of the Duke of Monmouth's rebel army slaughtered on the same moor in 1685, stories of mermaids, and ghostly figures all competing with Arthur for their place in the story books. And what of the smugglers? Dark nights, crashing sea, pinpricks of lanterns bobbing along rocky paths, silent boats gliding furtively through the black waves of intrigue and deception.

Creeping out of the boot and in an easterly direction, the character again changes. The sweeping plains of Salisbury, the magnificent New Forest, Dorchester and Thomas Hardy country, and on into Hampshire, home of the great naval base Portsmouth. Britain's indomitable antiquity is central to her fabric and Wiltshire is host to swirling mists of pre-history, the great white chalk horses, Stonehenge, Avebury, Silbury Hill; silent spectators on our present times, their secrets held tight. Travelling north and soon the echoes of pre-history turn to the rhetoric of Shakespeare and the muted cry of long past battles. This is the 'cockpit of England', the 'heart of England' and the birthplace of the great Elizabethan playwright. Across the lands of the South Midlands battles were fought in the incessant struggle for power. This area is also the very middle of England; an ancient cross outside Coventry marks the spot.

Down towards London and the South-East: the manicured lawns of Buckinghamshire, Berkshire and Surrey, beech woods of golden yellow, soft swelling green hills and the garden county – Kent. This is a gentle countryside of quiet beauty and ripe, productive farm land: fruit and hops, conical oast houses unique in form and appeal. A quiet belt of semi-rural respite from the loud hammering of Britain's largest and most famous city – London. Bright lights, fast business, retail, commerce, entertainment, music and laughter – London is host to a seething energy, a stream of movement, conscious thought and consequential actions, but also boasts some of the most magnificent architectural buildings of history and of the future. As with so much of Britain, London was established by the Romans, who have

left their mark from one end of the country to the other. Their planning, building and development shaped the country, her cities, roads and history of trading. They trod paths that had been worn before them by man's ancestors and laid the foundations for future peoples.

Today Britain is a country as rich and diverse in culture, history and landscape as any. Every corner, secret or otherwise, of this small island has something to offer; a visual feast of colour, landscape and atmosphere. From a splash of bright sun shining on water, green trees reflected, to the soaring spire of a Gothic cathedral, pearly white, uplifting, a feat of manpowered engineering; a crumbling castle, proud with the memories of once-great walls to silent, watchful, strange stones from pre-history; there is no single defining characteristic for Britain, she is the finished masterpiece, a canvas of many different brushstrokes.

Scotland

A WORLD APART FROM ENGLAND, SCOTLAND REMAINS DEFIANTLY SCOTTISH IN EVERY WAY, FROM HER DIALECT, CUSTOMS, CULTURE AND LANDSCAPE, THERE IS NO MISTAKING THE PROUD AND ENDURING BEARING OF THIS ANCIENT LAND.

With no significant border, except for the Cheviot Hills, one passes from England to Scotland with little ceremony, but on arrival the impact of Scotland is immediate and profound. Divided into the daunting and breathtaking Highlands, and the tamer Lowlands, Scotland is full of change and surprise. The Lowlands form swelling hills; vistas of green, tabletop fields dotted with sheep and still lochs, woodland, salmon-filled rivers and magnificent ruined abbeys; the romantic landscape of Sir Walter Scott and Robert Burns. Whereas the Lowlands are pretty and calm, the Highlands are sweepingly dramatic. Awe-inspiring, possessing fierce natural beauty, this area is home to vast panoramic scenes, towering mountains, roaring rivers, cascading waterfalls and colonies of wildlife found nowhere else. Castles and crumbling churches, forgotten abbeys, tiny crofter's houses and ancient burial mounds are scattered through the land; small handprints of man's presence since prehistoric times.

From this small corner of wild beauty has issued forth a procession of great artists, writers, poets, philosophers, scientists, sportsmen and warriors; a noble contingent reflective of their majestic birthplace.

Mam Ratagan Pass
ROSS-SHIRE

The air is clear and icy fresh, trees a riot of gold, the still, deep waters of Loch Duich vibrant blue turning to purple; the scene from the high Mam Ratagan Pass is one of breathtaking artistic inspiration. The imposing Five Sisters of the Kintail Mountains hunch to the east, their smaller siblings framing the long banks of Loch Duich. To the west Loch Duich joins with Loch Alsh and Loch Long, a spot marked by the hauntingly picturesque and historic Eilean Donnan Castle.

Traigh Mor Beach
ISLE OF BARRA

The Isle of Barra is referred to as 'Jewel of the Hebrides', and with its scenic coastline and rich, historic culture it is easy to see why. The beach of Traigh Mor on the northern peninsular of the island is especially captivating, with its smooth, silvery sands and wild beauty. Famous for its fine cockles, the area was also home to Compton Mackenzie, author of the book *Whisky Galore*: a satirical tale of a whisky-laden ship, wrecked off the neighbouring coast of the island of Eriskay.

The Prince's Monument
LOCH SHIEL, GLENFINNAN

Set against a backdrop of magnificent proportions the Prince's Monument stands in solitary defiance, an enduring bookmark in the bloody history of the Stuarts. It was here that Bonnie Prince Charlie, character of fact, fantasy and romance, raised his father's standard on 19 August 1745, marking the start of his campaign to restore the exiled Stuarts to the throne. The kilted statue, designed by the Scottish architect James Gillespie Graham, overlooks the quiet grandeur of Loch Shiel and St Finnan's Isle, the burial ground of the MacDonalds.

Towards Eigg and Rhum

GLENUIG BAY, MOIDART

One small figure in a landscape and suddenly the insignificance of the human element becomes apparent. This is the coast of Scotland at its best – sparkling, monumental and staggeringly beautiful. The islands of Eigg and Rhum in the distance form part of the Small Islands. Rhum, the largest island, has had the sea eagle re-introduced to its habitat, and is home to a wide range of wildlife and plants. In the middle of the island rise the Rum Cuillin Mountains, the remains of an ancient volcano.

Duart Castle

TOROSAY, ISLE OF MULL

What better way to cool off than in the refreshing waters of the Sound of Mull? Highland cattle's thick coats keep them well-protected against the harsh Scottish winters, but equally prove a little warm in the heat of the summer sun. The historic Duart Castle provides a picturesque background and dominates over the surrounding waters. The ancient building has been in the Maclean family since it was built in the thirteenth century, and seen many a colourful, treacherous family feud in its time.

Gylen Castle
ISLE OF KERRERA

The battle-scarred ruins of Gylen Castle have a picturesque beauty, appearing organically part of their landscape; a statement of a time gone by, a time of warfare, plundering and tragic loss of life. The sheer loveliness of the breathtaking views from Gylen and the tranquillity of the setting is absorbing, and at odds with the small castle's sad history. Just 60 years after it was built in the 1580s it was ransacked, burnt and the occupants slaughtered in an act of cowardice and mindless violence.

Buchan Ness Lighthouse
BODDAM, ABERDEENSHIRE

Three miles (5 km) north up the rocky coastline from Boddam is Peterhead, the busy fishing town that is the easternmost point of Scotland. During the nineteenth century Peterhead's fishing industries were growing rapidly, necessitating the construction of a lighthouse to guide boats safely through this treacherous portion of the North Sea. The Buchan Ness Lighthouse was built in 1827 by the engineer Robert Stevenson, grandfather of the famous novelist Robert Louis Stevenson, and was the first in Scotland to be equipped with a flashing light.

Dunnottar Castle

STONEHAVEN, ABERDEENSHIRE

Dunnottar Castle looms ghostlike through the morning mists, appearing and disappearing in a haze of soft light and water. The castle is surrounded on three sides by the crashing sea, and sits atop a high, rocky outcrop. Seagulls wheel amongst the ruined ramparts, their shrieks an echo of ancient bloodletting and battle. Dunnottar was the last castle in Scotland to hold out against Cromwell's army, famously enduring an eight-month siege during which the Scottish crown jewels were kept safe deep within the castle's walls.

Edradour Distillery

PITLOCHRY, PERTHSHIRE

Edradour holds the distinction of being Scotland's smallest distillery; perhaps 'most scenic' should be added too. It is hidden in the Highlands, tucked back in a glen in the hills above Pitlochry, and calls itself the last original 'farm' distillery in Perthshire. Amazingly, the entire operation is run by just three men who handcraft their whisky using traditional skills passed down through the generations. Edradour is regarded by many as being the finest and creamiest single-malt whisky in the world.

Loch Lomond

DUMBARTONSHIRE

The mirror surface of Loch Lomond casts near perfect reflections of the gently swaying boats. This is one of the largest Scottish lochs, and perhaps the most beautiful. The indigo waters, home to trout, pike and powan, stretch for 23 miles (37 km), punctuated by a series of tiny islands; during the fifth century these became a place of refuge for Irish missionaries. At the south end of the loch, verdant green pastures roll away from the shore, while to the north, wooded cliffs rise dramatically.

Princes Street

EDINBURGH

The buzzing Princes Street is the main vein of Edinburgh; alive, vibrant and cosmopolitan. It was built in the second half of the eighteenth century by the Hanoverian king, George III. Originally it was named St Giles, after the patron saint of Edinburgh, but the king objected and it was renamed in honour of his sons. The south side of Princes Street is lined with gardens, monuments and an uninterrupted view of the medieval Edinburgh Castle, while the north side boasts a parade of retail outlets.

TAVERN
THE SHIP TAVERN
THE SCOTTISH FISHERIES MUSEUM
THE GIFT SHOP
FR.958

Anstruther Harbour
EAST NEUK, FIFE

There is a clarity of light found in Scotland that enriches the palette of every scene. This view of Astruther Harbour is no exception; the vibrant juxtaposition of blue, white and red makes this an artist's dream. Just 50 years ago this harbour would have been packed tight with boats – one could have walked across them from one side of the harbour to the other. Fishing was the main industry here, but with the disappearance of the herring shoals from the North Sea, the fishing fleets too have decreased.

Loch Awe
ARGYLL

The dramatic Pass of Brander above Loch Awe shows nature's beauty at her most sublime. The sheer scale of this feature is defined by the matchbox-sized cars weaving along the loch-side road. This wild place has been the scene of many battles, the ruined castles along her banks a haunting testament; in 1308 Robert the Bruce used the pass to attack the Clan MacDougall. The north end of the loch is dominated by Ben Cruachan Mountain, below which are the impressive Falls of Cruachan.

St Abbs

BERWICKSHIRE

There is one road that leads into, and out of, St Abbs; the small and wholly unspoilt fishing village has retained its charm and rural loveliness. The crystal waters and rugged coastline around the village make this a destination for hikers, people seeking peace and quiet, and scuba divers. St Abbs is regarded as one of the top diving destinations in Britain, with dramatic underwater scenery, shipwrecks, and marine life rarely found in the North Sea, such as the wolf fish and the bolocera anemone.

River Tweed

LADYKIRK, BERWICKSHIRE

Berwick-Upon-Tweed sits on the border between Scotland and England. The town has, over the years, been gripped in the throes of many a territorial battle. Once Scotland's largest port, it was finally proclaimed English in 1482 after having changed hands 13 times. The great River Tweed flows through Berwick and roughly follows the borderline between the two countries. The river is privy to several impressive bridges such as this one; finished in the twentieth century, it is a statement of strength and monumentality.

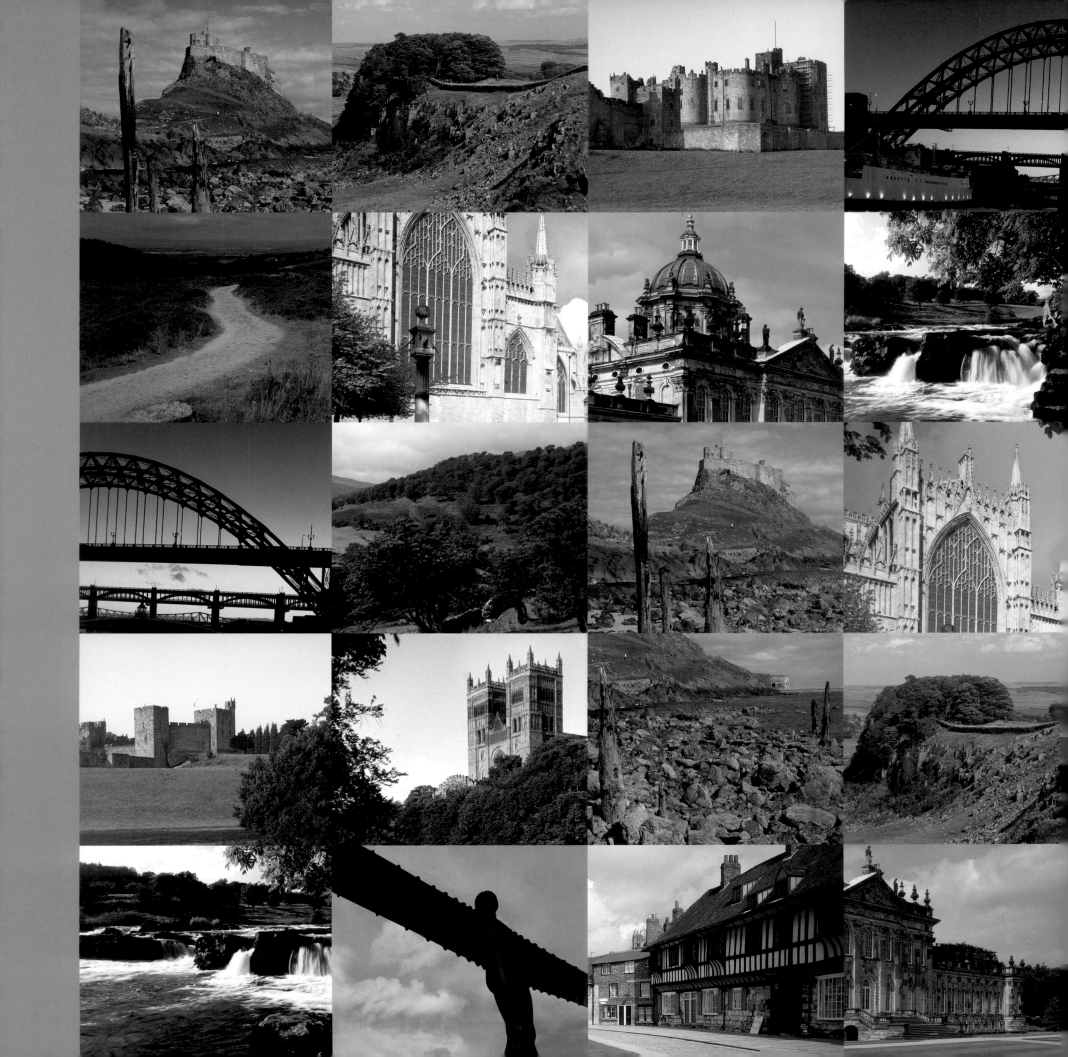

North-East England

Stretching from Northumbria, nestled against the Scottish border, to Sheffield knocking on the door of the Midlands, this corridor of land forms the indomitable North-East of England.

Some two thousand years ago, the Romans moved in and claimed some of the most productive and wildly beautiful landscape in Britain. Today, Hadrian's Wall, the most impressive of Britain's Roman relics, snakes in ruins across the undulating backbone of the land, an ancient barricade and a reminder of the turbulent and bloody past played out on the windswept reaches of the North.

Bordered to the west by the Pennines, the North-East is home to a highly dramatic landscape that makes it one of the most popular destinations for hikers, birdwatchers and those seeking solitude. This part of England is rich in the ruined monuments of times and people past. Great castles such as Castle Howard and Helmsley Castle loom through rolling mists, while the shimmering skeletons of ancient buildings such as Bolton Abbey pepper the haunting landscape.

The North-East is a landscape of exhilarating space, from the stalwart peaks of the Pennines and the roll of the Yorkshire Dales to the sweeping moorlands of heather, home to grouse and the wheeling curlew.

Lindisfarne Castle

NORTHUMBERLAND

Lindisfarne Castle stands sentry over its small kingdom of Holy Island. The castle was built in 1549 using stones from the skeleton of the nearby ruined abbey, and was designed as a fortress against the marauding Scots and their allies the French. By the 1900s the castle had fallen into ruins, and in 1902 it was bought by Edward Hudson, founder of *Country Life* magazine. He commissioned the architect Sir Edwin Lutyens to restore the castle and in 1968 it was taken over and preserved by the National Trust.

Hadrian's Wall

NORTHUMBERLAND

Built around AD 120 at the order of the Roman Emperor Hadrian, this impressive barricade snaked its way for 73 miles (117 km) from Wallsend-on-Tyne to the Soloway Firth. The wall was a fantastic feat of engineering, constructed of stone in the eastern part and turf to the west, with a sophisticated system of defensive ditches running its length. Not just a wall, the structure incorporated 17 large forts, smaller forts and watch towers and was garrisoned by infantry and cavalry. It remained in use until AD 383.

Alnwick Castle

NORTHUMBERLAND

This impressive medieval castle sits on a twelfth-century site and has been home to the powerful Percys, Earls and Dukes of Northumberland since 1309. Through the Middle Ages Alnwick was partially ruined during bloody border warfare, and was not restored until the eighteenth century. Described by the current Duke of Northumberland as 'Windsor of the North', the castle now houses stunning state rooms with works by Canaletto, Titian and Van Dyck. Recently Alnwick has provided the backdrop for two of the popular Harry Potter films.

Tyne Bridge
TYNE & WEAR

Newcastle-Upon-Tyne grew from humble beginnings; first serving as an outpost for the Romans, it has continued to develop and is now the capital of the North. Despite massive industrial expansion, this great city remains one of the most attractive of northern cities, due in large part to the town planning of Victorian architect John Dobson. Newcastle is a city of bridges, with five historic and beautiful bridges spanning the Tyne; each different but magnificent, they are an inspiring gateway to the heart of the city.

Angel of the North
TYNE & WEAR

The evocative silhouette of the Angel of the North rising from her hillside site, welcoming you to Tyneside, is a compelling mixture of ancient mysticism and modernism. The Angel herself is a celebration of clean line and simple, monumental form; the site a reclaimed former colliery pit. She was designed by the visionary contemporary artist Antony Gormley OBE and was unveiled in 1998. At 65 feet (20 m) high, and with a 177-foot (54-m) wingspan, she is thought to be the largest angel sculpture in the world.

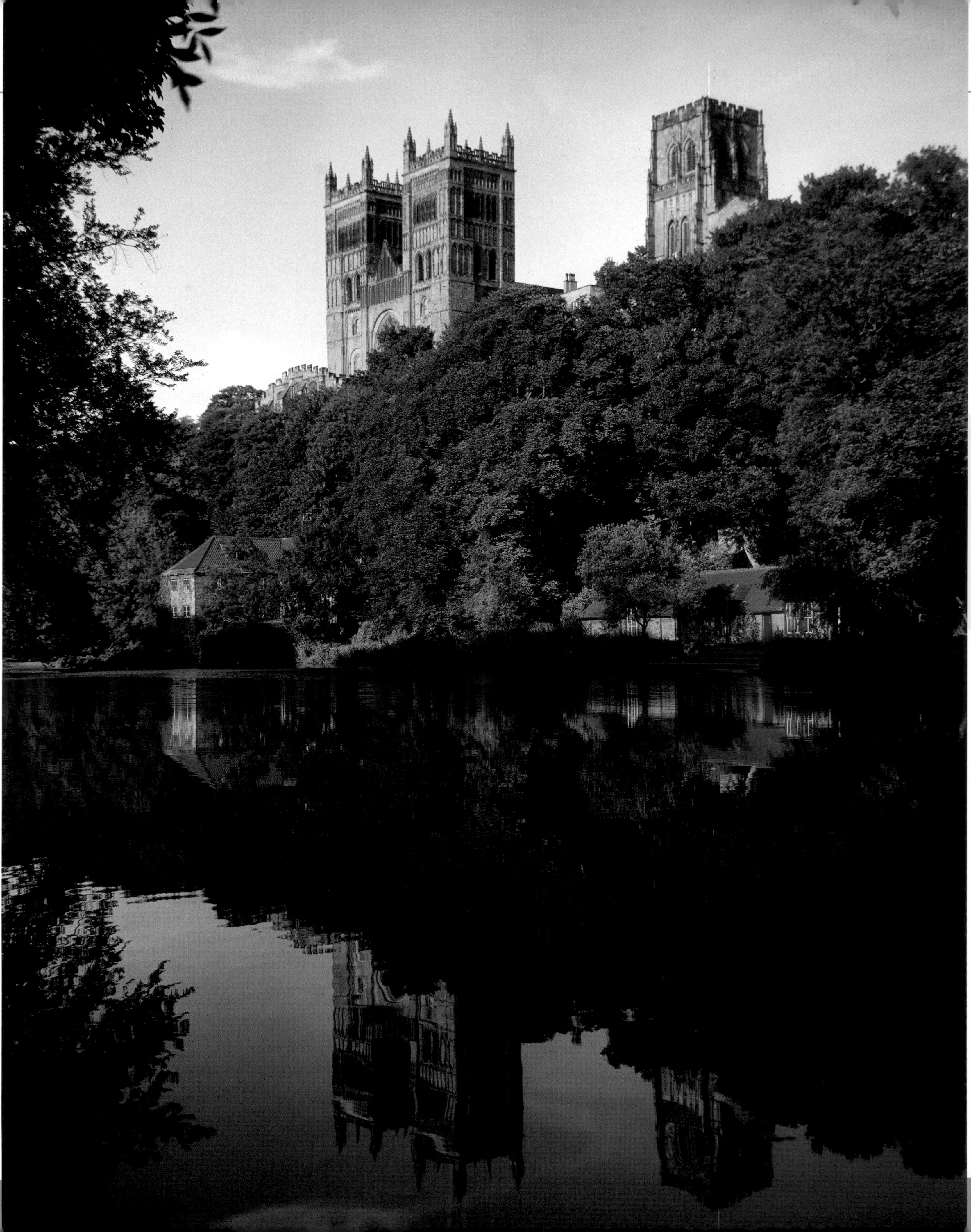

Durham Cathedral

COUNTY DURHAM

'Grey towers of Durham yet well I love thy mixed and massive piles, half church of God, half castle 'gainst the Scot': the words of Sir Walter Scott, inscribed on a plaque on the Prebends Bridge overlooking the magnificent Durham Cathedral. William de St Carileph commissioned the Norman cathedral in 1093, building it on the site of an existing Saxon church. The cathedral sits on its rocky site, surrounded on three sides by the River Wear, and next to the great Durham Castle, which dates back to *c.* 1070.

North York Moors

YORKSHIRE

Far in the distance shimmers the village of Osmotherly, across miles of wide-open Yorkshire Moors. This is a place of myth and legend, superstition and great tales, a barren, rugged landscape of adventure and history. The Moors are crossed by the Cleveland Way and the Lyke Wake Walk, two long trails that wind through many miles of stunning countryside, historical sites and abundant wildlife. This wild country was the birthplace of Captain James Cook, one of the greatest explorers of all time.

York Minster

YORKSHIRE

York is one of the most beautiful cities in Britain and is home to York Minster, the finest and largest of the Gothic cathedrals in Northern Europe. The Minster has an ancient, turbulent history, and has been destroyed and rebuilt since Roman times – remains of the Roman settlement on which the cathedral was built are visible in the undercroft. Next to the Minster is the fifteenth-century, half-timbered St William's College, originally home to the cathedral chantry priests.

Castle Howard

YORKSHIRE

The magnificent Castle Howard sits in a stately parkland setting; this is surely one of the most palatial of country seats. The house was designed in the early 1700s by the notable architect Sir John Vanbrugh and his assistant Nicholas Hawksmoor for the third Earl of Carlisle, and is home to an impressive collection of antique furniture. The grounds are as hauntingly beautiful as the house and include a circular mausoleum designed by Hawksmoor and the Temple of The Four Winds, designed by Vanbrugh.

Waterfall on River Wharfe

YORKSHIRE

The sun shines on the water, a perfect summer day steeped in the rushing song of these waterfalls, endlessly churning and tumbling with white froth. The River Wharfe is one of Yorkshire's most popular destinations for canoeists, wending its way from the Yorkshire Dales to the River Ouse, but it is not without its adventures, as these falls can testify. The river cuts a swathe through the green countryside with stunning views of the Wharfe Valley, and offers fantastic brown-trout fishing.

Yorkshire Dales

YORKSHIRE

The Yorkshire Dales are one of Britain's great areas of natural beauty and a favourite spot for hikers and outdoor-sports enthusiasts. There is a little bit of everything here, from gentle walks for nature lovers to extreme hikes for the more adventurous. This view across to Coverdale, one of the smaller dales, is typical of the outstanding beauty of the area. Vibrant green fields give way to rolling hills, patchworked with a crisscross of low stone walls; this is Yorkshire at her most picturesque.

North-West England

FROM THE SUBLIME SPLENDOUR OF CUMBRIA AND THE LAKE DISTRICT, THROUGH THE ROMANCE OF LANCASHIRE AND THE COSMOPOLITAN METROPOLIS OF MERSEYSIDE, TO THE ANCIENT TOWN OF CHESTER, NORTH-WEST ENGLAND HOLDS A UNIQUELY DIVERSE APPEAL.

Bordered by sea to the west, the rugged Pennine Mountains to the east, Scotland to the north and Wales to the south, the North-West is full of its own character and appeal. The Romans first settled the city that would become Chester in AD 79, fiercely guarding their fertile and productive new territory from the marauding Welsh. From these ancient roots, the surrounding area emerged as a leader in industry, agriculture and tourism. Although associated with cotton mills and coal mining, Lancashire today is better known for her astonishing landscape, which encompasses the wild, untamed glory of Pendle Hill and the majestic Forest of Bowland.

The North-West is a place of extraordinary beauty, ranging from the soft, sandy coastlines of Cumbria to the rolling farmlands of the Cheshire Plains, from the tranquil lakes of Lancashire to the hubbub of Blackpool and her famous illuminations. This small corner of Britain is home to some of the most inspiring and surprising scenery in the country.

Castlerigg Stone Circle
CUMBRIA

Bathed in the haunting glow of the dying sun, this ancient stone circle stands proud and mysterious; the secret of its foundation and history remain a permanent, irretrievable enigma. The setting is edged by the dramatic rim of mountains, a jagged skyline border to a flat plateau of green. The silhouette of the stones seems to echo the mountains; the significance of the site forever just beyond reach. A bird wheels and the sun slips away, all things in transit apart from the solemn, time-enduring circle itself.

Friar's Crag
CUMBRIA

John Ruskin described the scene of Friar's Crag jutting into Derwentwater as one of the three most beautiful scenes in Europe, and it is easy to see why. Ruskin had a long association with this area, and he is commemorated by a simple memorial on Friar's Crag. Derwentwater is one of the gorgeous lakes of the Lake District, and is particularly known for its evocative atmosphere and haunting, moody light. Every vista is as though taken straight from a canvas, each a work of art in itself.

The Langdale Pikes
CUMBRIA

In the heart of the Lake District is the Langdale Valley, a lush valley of green with sweeping views, topped by the imposing Langdale Pikes. These three rocky peaks are known as Pike of Stickle, Harrison Stickle and Pavey Ark. This is the country of mountains, valleys and water, and although the Langdale Pikes are smaller than some of their neighbours, they are just as impressive. Seen here from Chapel Stile, the Langdale Pikes can also be viewed from across Lake Windermere, which is itself magnificent.

Fell Foot Park

CUMBRIA

The huge Lake Windermere cuts a watery slash through the Lake District; to the west lies Grizedale Forest Park and to the east an expanse of beautiful country leading down towards the town of Kendal. On the southern shores of Windermere is Fell Foot Park, a pretty Victorian park with manicured gardens and fantastic views across the lake. Boating and recreation is primary here; this is a place to relax, unwind, and enjoy a gentle day's sailing, savouring the spectacular views across Lake Windermere.

Ashness Bridge

CUMBRIA

Ashness Bridge, or the Old Packhorse Bridge, spans a riotous brook that wends its way towards to the impressive Derwentwater. In the distance, the imposing craggy peaks of Skiddaw scowl down on the landscape, throwing a shadow across Keswick to the east, Bassenthwaite Lake to the west and Derwentwater to the south. The weary traveller of old stepping across Ashness Bridge has been replaced by the enthusiastic tourist; this has become a very popular trail, and is a beautiful scene at any time of the year.

Ullswater

CUMBRIA

William Wordsworth wrote when describing Ullswater that it was 'the happiest combination of beauty and grandeur, that any of the lakes affords'. This lake, in the north-east corner of the Lake District, is the second longest lake in the area, and snakes its way through the most dramatic scenery of great fells, woods and a ring of mountains at its southern end. The lake has attracted settlers for centuries, and takes its name from an early Norse settler, L'Ulf.

Blackpool Tower

LANCASHIRE

Soaring 518 feet (153 m) into the air, Lancashire's Blackpool Tower dominates the miles of promenade. It is even more spectacular at night, when the tower forms part of the famous Blackpool Illuminations; it glows in the darkness, an elegant but opulent beacon of entertainment. The tower was begun in 1891 and is typical of the Victorian style of measured extravagance. At that time Blackpool was fast becoming one of the most popular seaside resort towns, a position that it has held for over 100 years.

Albert Dock
MERSEYSIDE

Liverpool's Albert Dock is a testament to the powers of restoration and commercialism in the current climate of cultural and economic interest. The docks were officially opened in 1846 and were a huge achievement in the history of dock engineering. Liverpool's flourishing trading importance saw the docks filled with precious cargoes from all over the world. By 1972 shipping here had diminished and the docks were closed. After a massive restoration process the site has been turned into a thriving cosmopolitan centre of entertainment and cultural heritage.

The Pumphouse Inn
MERSEYSIDE

The Albert Dock has been turned into a conservation area to preserve the fascinating history of Liverpool's emergence as a major port. The fortunes of the city are intrinsically bound to the development of her docks; it was the advent of the steamship in the 1840s that really saw Liverpool's trading take off. The Pumphouse Inn was built around 1878 and served as the pump house for the docks. It has since been converted to a pub, but retains some of its original character.

River Dee

CHESHIRE

The River Dee winds its way past the ancient scenic city of Chester, heading out towards the Irish Sea. The wide, blue ribbon passing Chester is spanned by many bridges, but only one footbridge – the elegant white Queen's Park Suspension Bridge. The bridge was originally built in 1852 in conjunction with a development of city suburbs across the river. In 1922 the bridge was demolished and a new bridge was built to the designs of Charles Greenwood. The new bridge was expertly restored in 1998.

Roman City Walls

CHESHIRE

The Romans first established their camp of Deva on the site of modern Chester in AD 79, and set about construction of the monumental enclosing wall in an effort to keep the marauding Welsh at bay. This is one of the best surviving examples of Roman ramparts, with much of the original wall still very much in evidence; some 'modern' additions were made to it in the Middle Ages! In spring, the base of the wall comes alive with the brilliant yellow of daffodils.

Wales

WALES IS A COUNTRY SHROUDED IN THE MISTS OF LEGEND AND MYSTERY, AND ITS SUBLIME BEAUTY HAS REMAINED LARGELY UNDISTURBED BY MAN.

Wales has a character uniquely her own – from the soft, lilting language of her people to the rise and plunge of her mountain ranges; the stone and slate farmhouses pressed into the landscape, to the sheep on the open moorland; the rush of her many rivers, to the dense forests peopled with ancient trees. To the north lie the soaring peaks of Snowdonia, home to Mount Snowdon, and to the south the Brecon Beacons and Black Mountains; running between the two are the Cambrian Mountains, a natural barricade between Wales and England. Dotted with arcane ruins, fortresses, castles and prehistoric sites bearing the mark of the Romans, the Celts, the Normans, the Christians and the Druids, Wales' far-reaching history is evident in her landscape.

With vast areas populated solely by colonies of wild birds and animals, carpets of jewel-like flowers in the spring and salmon-filled rivers, Wales is a sanctuary for the most weary of souls, a place that is uplifting and gloriously unspoilt.

The Snowdon Horseshoe

SNOWDONIA

Nestled in the north-west corner of Wales is the great Snowdonia, a national park region of extraordinary beauty – a wild, rugged, natural loveliness that is at once inviting and challenging. The narrow ridge of the Snowdon Horseshoe can be seen here across the flat waters of Lake Mymbyr. This is a walker's paradise, so long as you do not suffer from vertigo! The land falls steeply away on either side of the trail that runs along the top of the Horseshoe, but from here the views are tremendous.

The Snowdon Railway
SNOWDONIA

Mount Snowdon is the highest point in Britain south of the Scottish borders; its majestic and daunting peak makes it a top destination for experienced climbers from all over the world. A less strenuous way to see some of the spectacular scenery in this area is by taking the Snowdon Railway. Starting at the small village of Llanberis at the base of Snowdon, the train chugs to within 66 feet (20 m) of the summit; a dramatic and scenic ride that is not for the faint-hearted!

Harlech Castle
GWYNEDD

Perched high above the surrounding landscape, this spectacular fortress dominates the skyline and appears to have evolved seamlessly from the rock on which it sits. The castle was commissioned in 1283 by Edward I during his conquest of Wales, and was built in record time at vast expense. Harlech has a history steeped in blood and violence, and was continually plundered and raided; it was coined the 'Castle of Lost Causes' and was the last Royalist stronghold in Wales during the Civil War.

Daffodils in Bodnant Garden
CONWY

The glorious yellow of the daffodils in Bodnant Garden signal the first step into spring, and precede the riot of colour that will follow as each sunny day coaxes another bloom to unfurl. Bodnant is a garden jewel; set high above the River Conwy and with outstanding views towards Snowdonia, it never ceases to amaze. The garden was formally designed in the early 1900s by the second Lord Aberconway, although sections of the garden and much of the tree planting began some years earlier.

Aberystwyth Harbour
CARDIGANSHIRE

Aberystwyth sits overlooking the Cardigan Bay to the west, and is backed by the expansive and beautiful scenery of Cardiganshire. This is one of the least populated of the Welsh counties and is home to sweeping moorlands, mountains and forests. Aberystwyth is the cultural jewel of this backdrop, and boasts a lively town life that revolves around the picturesque harbour and the University of Wales Aberystwyth. Its clean beaches, boating and cultural history of the town make it a favourite destination for tourists.

Brecon Beacons
POWYS

Green fields of cotton-wool sheep, a bright sunny day, blue sky and pristine clouds billowing from behind the ridge of the Brecon Becons – what a beautiful combination of natural ingredients. Seen from the historic town of Brecon, the Beacons form a soaring perimeter, sandwiched between the Black Mountain range that runs from Carmarthenshire in the west to Monmouthshire in the east. The peaks of the Brecon Beacons are only accessible by foot, but the walk is worth it – the views from the top are stunning.

St David's Cathedral
PEMBROKESHIRE

St David's Cathedral rises majestically out of the landscape, the great white stone structure visible for miles, stark against the gorgeous backdrop of green fields and trees. The cathedral – located in Britain's smallest city – was built on the site of the sixth-century monastery of St David, who died in AD 589, and so occupies an area of ancient religious history. The present cathedral was begun in 1181; in 1793 John Nash rebuilt the west front and in 1862 Sir George Gilbert Scott began a lengthy restoration of the building.

Stack Rocks at St Govan's Head

PEMBROKESHIRE

The Stack Rocks, or Elegug Stacks, are two razors of limestone that poke up out of the sea just off the rugged coast of Pembrokeshire. Elegug, named after the Welsh word for guillemot, is a refuge for sea birds and is densely populated by its namesake, as well as kittiwakes, fulmars, razorbills and black-backed gulls. St Govan's Head, the last point of land before the Stack Rocks, is famous for the tiny thirteenth-century, one-room chapel to St Govan that clings precariously to the cliff edge.

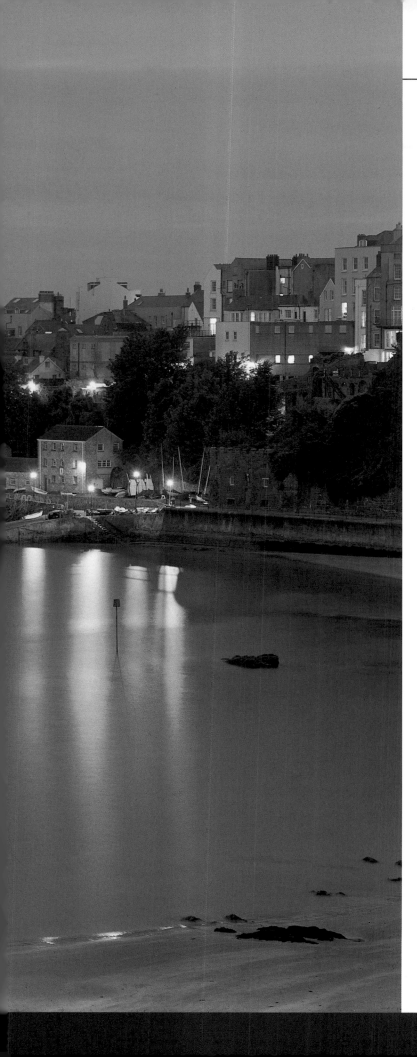

Tenby Harbour

PEMBROKESHIRE

The lights reflect in the water, as flat and calm as a mirror on this beautiful still evening. Tenby Harbour by night is a magical place, while by day it is a picturesque and busy centre, backed by pretty, pastel-coloured buildings, and looking out towards Carmarthen Bay and Caldey Island. The quiet, azure sea of summer can be a whipping, turbulent rage in the winter, with huge waves crashing against the harbour; a different kind of beauty in the chill of the year's end.

Cardiff Millennium Stadium

GLAMORGAN

Wales is a country associated with beautiful landscapes, sheep and rural tranquillity, but it is also responsible for a formidable wealth of sporting talent. It is fitting then that the Millennium Stadium, a technological wonder, should have been built in Cardiff. The stadium was opened in late 1999 and is an example of cutting-edge architecture, with its retractable roof, covered walkways, recycling irrigation system and removable turf pitch. Yet more dramatic is the sheer elegance of the design, the aesthetic sensibility and the thoroughly modern statement that it makes.

Severn Bridge

MONMOUTHSHIRE

Stretching into the distance in an iridescent haze of bright light, the Severn Bridge appears unearthly, hovering above the great ribbon of the River Severn like the fine strands of a spider's web. To the untrained eye, it seems unbelievable that the bridge could support itself but, like spider silk, the graceful bridge supports belie their formidable strength. Since its opening in 1966 it has made the Welsh near neighbours of the Forest of Dean and Bristol, transporting millions of cars every year across the Severn Estuary.

Heart of England

THE HEART OF ENGLAND BEATS TO A DIFFERING RHYTHM; THE SLOW PASTORAL MARCH OF HEREFORDSHIRE AND WORCESTERSHIRE, THE THUNDER OF GLOUCESTERSHIRE WITH HER HORSERACING AND EVENTING, THE MEASURED TOLL OF SHAKESPEARE'S LAND, WARWICKSHIRE, THE ACADEMIC PULSE OF OXFORDSHIRE AND HER LOVELY STONE ARCHITECTURE, THE HAMMER OF INDUSTRY THROUGH THE WEST MIDLANDS AND THE SLOW, EASY TEMPO OF BEAUTIFUL DERBYSHIRE, NOTTINGHAMSHIRE AND SHROPSHIRE.

This middle England encompasses landscapes as wild and divergent as the histories played out here. To the north sits the rugged face of the Peak District, to the south the impressive Cotswold Hills, their quaint limestone villages tucked into lush green farmland, behind mellow stone walls. Herefordshire, the land of the cider apple and the famous Hereford cow, rests in the shadow of the Welsh mountains to the west, while Oxford with her yellowed stone buildings and the tumbling River Charwell, looks east.

Through England's heart winds a stream of steady waters, for this is an area rich in rivers and the birthplace of the great River Thames. Sparkling waters flowing through a verdant landscape, cattle and sheep grazing, houses set round a village green and traditional pubs – as diverse as this area's landscape is, it remains quintessentially, beautifully British.

Peak Forest
DERBYSHIRE

Right in the heart of Britain lies the Peak District, 540 square miles (1,398 square km) of uninterrupted glorious country, and Britain's first National Park. Sweeping away as far as the eye can see is the lush green of this fertile landscape, from the top of the Rushup Edge down towards the small village of Peak Forest. This small, stone farm nestled into the hillside is typical of the region: picturesque, at one with the scenery and a busy pocket of rural life.

Chatsworth House
DERBYSHIRE

In 1843, during his trip to Russia for the coronation of Tsar Nicholas, the sixth Duke of Devonshire saw the impressive fountain at Peterhof. On his return to Chatsworth he commissioned Sir Joseph Paxton to design his own fountain to surpass one he had seen in Russia, and to surprise the Tsar when he visited. The massive project involved digging the lake and building the fountain; men worked through the night to complete it on time. Although the Tsar actually never made his promised trip to the house, the fountain was still named in his honour.

River Wye Viaduct
DERBYSHIRE

The great Victorian viaduct cuts a bright path through the middle of this panorama of sedate countryside. It was built to provide an efficient rail link between Buxton and Bakewell but met with heavy criticism when it was opened, most notably from the venerated Victorian architect and critic John Ruskin. The River Wye flows underneath, winding its way towards the Derwent at Rowsley. This is one of the prettiest of British rivers and is a favourite spot for salmon and trout anglers, as well as hikers.

Sherwood Forest
NOTTINGHAMSHIRE

In the north-east of Nottinghamshire lies the remains of Sherwood Forest, the one-time magnificent royal hunting grounds thought to have been established by William the Conqueror. Sherwood is, however, better known for its association with the famous folk hero Robin Hood. The great oak trees of the forest provided Robin and his merry men with shelter and protection from the wicked Sheriff of Nottingham. The forest is now greatly reduced and these blasted oaks serve as a poignant reminder of the frailty of our natural wonders.

Robin Hood Statue
NOTTINGHAMSHIRE

Robin Hood is one of the most enduring and traditional of the 'people's heroes', and also one of the most mystical. The tales of Robin Hood cross over between fact and fiction; some ballads claim that he lived in Sherwood Forest, some in Yorkshire's Barnsdale Forest. Through all the stories Robin retains his chivalry, dignity and grace, battling the rich on behalf of the poor and hounding the Sheriff of Nottingham. James Woodford's statue outside Nottingham Castle perfectly captures the brave character of Britain's favourite outlaw.

Iron Bridge
SHROPSHIRE

A boat glides gently towards the bridge, the faintest ripple left in its wake. This scene of quiet tranquillity belies the heavy industrialism that this area was subjected to during the Industrial Revolution. The Iron Bridge that spans the River Severn was built in 1779 and was the first example of cast iron being used for industrial architecture. The constantly shifting river banks and ensuing strain on the bridge has resulted in cracks, the first of which appeared in 1784, and it is in need of continual restoration and conservation.

Long Mynd
SHROPSHIRE

The Long Mynd, meaning 'Long Mountain', is a 10-mile (16-km) ridge of windswept hills, made up of some of the oldest rock to be found in Britain. This bleak ridge sits astride the Church Stretton Fault that formed roughly 550 million years ago during volcanic eruptions. Running along the top of the Long Mynd is an ancient pathway, the Port Way, and from here there are stunning views. This is an area full of history and is home to many prehistoric sites of interest.

Stokesay Castle
SHROPSHIRE

This fine manor house dates back to the twelfth century, the gabled half-timbering on the north tower added on later during the sixteenth century. Stokesay has one of the best and oldest-surviving examples of a great hall; the scene surely to feisty banquets, the air spiced with savoury smells, wood-smoke, roasting meat and warm bodies round the roaring fireplace. The house was built by Lawrence of Ludlow, a prosperous wool merchant, and was later fortified by the de Sayes family, from whom it takes its name.

Malvern Hills

WORCESTERSHIRE

The Malvern Hills rest on the western boundary of Worcestershire, commanding views across Gloucestershire, Worcestershire and Herefordshire. They roll across the country for about eight miles (13 km); soft, green and pastoral, they offer some of the best walks for hiking enthusiasts. At nearly 1,400 feet (427 m) Worcestershire Beacon is the highest point, with British Camp, the Iron-Age hill fort, a slightly lower hill. From here there are stunning views across the patchwork countryside of Worcestershire, stretching as far as the eye can see.

The Old Bull

WORCESTERSHIRE

This must be one of the Britain's best known and loved inns, at least for fans of Radio 4's *The Archers*. The charming, timber-framed building was the model for the Bull at Ambridge in *The Archers* serial; the pub sign features an irritable-looking Hereford. The Old Bull has a long history of its own, however, and in 1582 Shakespeare stayed there on his way to collect his marriage certificate in Worcester. The village of Inkberrow is a suitably historic backdrop to the Old Bull.

Hereford Cathedral
HEREFORDSHIRE

Standing serenely on the banks of the River Wye, Hereford Cathedral is a feast for the eyes. It is not only the predominantly Norman exterior that is so compelling, but also the interior, stunningly restored and home to two of Britain's greatest historic treasures; the Mappa Mundi, a medieval map of the world, is one of the finest ancient maps in Europe, and was painted by Richard of Haldingham around 1275, while the seventeenth-century Chained Library is the largest library of its kind in the world.

Coventry Cathedral
WARWICKSHIRE

The evocative image of old and new is one that has a profound effect on the senses. Bombing in Coventry in 1940 obliterated the original cathedral, which was immediately rebuilt by Sir Basil Spence as a modern symbol of hope. The new cathedral is a gallery for works by Graham Sutherland, John Piper, Epstein, Frink, John Hutton and Ralph Beyer. Two charred roof timbers from the old building form a poignant cross, crowning an altar of rubble; the old and new forever bound in a tapestry of human actions.

Warwick Castle

WARWICKSHIRE

Follow the River Avon around a bend and there, suddenly, is the breathtaking Warwick Castle, its reflection rippling on the surface of the water. An imposing vision of medieval splendour, the castle harbours a bloody and turbulent past, the scene of treachery and torture; a not unfamiliar history for Britain's great fortresses. Much of the interior was rebuilt during the seventeenth century, and then again in 1770 following a devastating fire. The grand exterior of the castle is matched by the handsome landscaped gardens, designed by the famous Capability Brown.

Shakespeare's Birthplace

WARWICKSHIRE

It is extraordinary that, over 400 years after his birth, William Shakespeare still holds the position of one of the most highly regarded playwrights of all time. This great contributor to the history of literature was born in Stratford-Upon-Avon, in this pretty, half-timbered house in Henley Street in 1564. From here Shakespeare's father, John, ran his successful business as a glove-maker and wool-dealer, eventually expanding the house to incorporate Joan Hart's Cottage, a single-bay building built on to the north-west end.

Anne Hathaway's Cottage

WARWICKSHIRE

This charming thatched home, located near Stratford-Upon-Avon, is the quintessential English country cottage. Flowers bursting with colour, birds singing, the smell of summer; the perfect place for William Shakespeare to court his future wife, Anne Hathaway. One can only wonder what poetic words of romance the young playwright used, words he perhaps drew on again for his plays. The couple were married in 1582 in the village of Temple Grafton, and shortly afterwards moved into Shakespeare's father's house in Stratford-Upon-Avon. Six months after their wedding, Anne produced their first child, Susanna.

Tewkesbury Abbey

GLOUCESTERSHIRE

The magnificent Tewkesbury Abbey dates back to the early twelfth century, and houses more medieval tombs than any other church in the country, with the exception of Westminster Abbey. According to notes by Shakespeare, one of the tombs holds the body of George, Duke of Clarence, who allegedly drowned in a butt of Malmsey wine!

The abbey also has an impressive Norman tower that soars 132 feet (40 m) into the sky, and an outstanding Norman arch of six orders on the west front.

River Severn
GLOUCESTERSHIRE

The simple but charming timbered cottage, with white-painted plaster or brickwork, is perhaps most evocative of the British country home. Here, standing serenely along the banks of the slow-moving River Severn, one of Britain's longest and most impressive rivers, these quaint cottages are picture-perfect, right down to their reflected facades. This is a Britain that is hard to beat; the sun shines, there is not a breath of wind and even the river seems still, all bound in a pervading trance of quiet and tranquillity.

The Promenade Gardens
GLOUCESTERSHIRE

Charles Dickens said of Cheltenham: 'Rarely have I seen such a place that so attracted my fancy'. It is undoubtedly one of the most elegant towns in Britain, with its smooth, polished Georgian houses and abundance of manicured parks. The town was first recognised as a spa town in 1719, and became fashionable as a retreat for the wealthy between 1790 and 1840. During this period, many fine buildings were built and today Cheltenham is regarded as one of the best examples of a Regency town in Britain.

Snowshill

GLOUCESTERSHIRE

The honeyed tones of Cotswold limestone, rolling green hills and riotous flowers make this area a visual delight. The small village of Snowshill is unspoilt and charming; small mellow houses crouch together, unpretentious yet beautiful in the simplicity of their design. A flash of bright sun, a gentle breeze and singing birds make this place a private Elysium. Two miles (3.2 km) outside the village is the Tudor Snowshill Manor, an eerie place of ghosts and history that adds to the slightly mysterious flavour of the village.

Oxford Spires

OXFORDSHIRE

With her majestic stone buildings and history steeped in refinement and academia, Oxford remains one of the jewels of Britain. The dreaming spires of the university's colleges soar skywards in a panorama as uplifting and lofty as the institution they enclose. The lively voice of debate, religious, political and cultural, echoes through the stones of her streets. Oxford, although now a fast-paced student town of shops, pubs and social activity, remains at her core entirely integral to the university, her history and culture shaped through the pursuit of knowledge.

Magdalen College
OXFORDSHIRE

'The most absolute tower in England.' These are the reputed words of James I when describing Magdalen College's Great Tower, which dominates the east entrance to Oxford. Every year on May 1, the college choir sings part of the college grace from the top of the tower – a moving experience to witness. Magdalen is regarded as the most attractive of the Oxford colleges; not only are the fifteenth century buildings ethereally beautiful but the college is set in 100 acres (40 hectares) of stunning parkland, alive with flowers and wildlife.

The Falkland Arms
OXFORDSHIRE

There is nothing quite so British as the traditional pub. The favoured watering hole for Britons over hundreds of years, the pub has a history almost as long as history itself. Nowhere in the world is the British pub equalled, and imitations are always poor. The Falkland Arms, which was named after Viscount Falkland, secretary to Charles I, dates back to the sixteenth century. This historic pub is everything a pub should be: traditional, welcoming, full of antique pub furniture and brasses, and with an excellent range of beers.

Henley Regatta

OXFORDSHIRE

A short stretch of the River Thames is home to the greatest, oldest and most famous river regatta in the world. Henley Royal Regatta was first held in 1839, and has taken place annually except during the First and Second World Wars. The race starts at Temple Island, home to James Wyatt's 1771 folly, and finishes a gruelling seven minutes later at Poplar Point. This is spectator sport, and the Henley enclosure is famous for its strict dress codes, champagne, Pimms, and strawberries with cream.

East Anglia

THE COASTLINE OF EAST ANGLIA CRUMBLES DEFIANTLY AGAINST THE RELENTLESS BARRAGE OF THE NORTH SEA, THE BEACHES AND COASTAL VILLAGES CONSTANTLY SHIFTING AND EVOLVING.

East Anglia is home to a largely flat landscape that affords incredible panoramic skies. Softened with gently swelling hills, the scenery is predominantly agricultural; patchwork fields of neat, brown, ploughed troughs and furrows, turning to the vibrant green of winter wheat, or soft golden barley and oats. Windmills stand sentry on the skyline, competing with the hundreds of churches that pepper East Anglia, their steeples rising from a misty landscape. Scenes from this rural idyll are reminiscent of seventeenth-century Dutch landscapes, and the influence of the Dutch here is often apparent, from the Dutch-gabled ends of houses to the drained marshlands of the Fens.

There is a peculiar, ethereal light in East Anglia that is unique to the area. For centuries artists have flocked here to capture that light on canvas; it is not unusual to stumble across tiny, thriving artistic communities settled around pretty village greens.

This is a place of unspoilt beauty that combines rural tranquillity with the excitement of horse-racing from Newmarket, the architectural splendour of Norwich Cathedral and Cambridge University, and the bustling fishing trade up and down the coastline.

Lincoln Cathedral
LINCOLNSHIRE

The magnificent, largely Gothic Lincoln Cathedral dominates the surrounding countryside from its position high on a limestone plateau. The Romans chose this site in AD 48 to establish a settlement – now Lincoln – due to its advantageous location. The cathedral was begun in 1185, and was built on the site of an earlier Norman church that was largely destroyed during an earthquake; to the west end are three of the original Norman portals, surmounted by a fantastic sculpted frieze dating back to *c*. 1145.

Coastal Scene
NORFOLK

On the northern face of East Anglia's distinctive 'bump' sits Cromer, home of the famously delicious Cromer crab. This is an area of rural charm, a small fishing village grown large recently on the strength of its pleasant beaches and the tourist industry. Despite this, Cromer still has the heart of a fishing community, and Cromer crab is sold up and down the coastline, and across the country. The town is presided over by the church of St Peter and St Paul, which boasts the tallest tower in Norfolk.

Happisburgh Beach

NORFOLK

The Norfolk coastline is notoriously wild and suffers a continual battering from the warring North Sea. The beaches and headlands are constantly changing, eroding and evolving into new vistas. Scattered across Happisburgh Beach are the skeletal remains of wooden sea defences built in the 1950s, and in 2002 the lifeboat ramp finally collapsed on to the beach. There is, nonetheless, a stark and admirable beauty to this ravaged coastline – one that is hard to find anywhere else, and that certainly demands our respect.

Pull's Ferry, River Wensum

NORFOLK

The ancient cathedral town of Norwich developed around a huge double bend in the stately River Wensum, which snakes its way through the heart of the town before joining the River Yare to the east. As a main route of trading and commerce, the river was crucial to Norwich's development. It was along the river that stone was carried to build the cathedral, passing under the fifteenth-century water gate, Pull's Ferry, before entering a canal to take the stone directly to the building site.

Great Bircham Windmill

NORFOLK

Great Bircham windmill speaks of the past, the traditional ways of farming life that were the basis for rural Norfolk's economy. Stately and serene, the windmill is a poignant symbol of agricultural heritage. Simultaneously, the combine harvester tells of the present; agriculture is still the prime industry here in the heart of Norfolk, but the pace has been stepped up. Great Bircham windmill is one of the finest remaining windmills in the country, and is still in working order.

Great Yarmouth

NORFOLK

The lively town of Great Yarmouth sits on a narrow peninsular of land, bordered by the River Yare on one side and the North Sea on the other. Today Yarmouth is the largest of the Norfolk coastal towns, and with her 15 miles (24 km) of sandy beaches and two piers she has become one of the most popular seaside resort destinations. Originally, however, Yarmouth's fortunes were built upon her herring industry and ship building, before the port turned to servicing the North Sea oil and gas operations.

Norfolk Broads

NORFOLK

The Norfolk and Suffolk Broads form the largest protected wetland in Britain, and are an area of outstanding natural beauty. The rivers, lakes, marshes and fens of these areas are home to a wide range of wildlife and birds rarely spotted elsewhere. Years ago the Broads were part of an important transport system, forming a web across East Anglia; now, however, they are a top destination for boating enthusiasts, drawn by the tranquil landscape and beautiful, unique light of this part of the country.

Bridge of Sighs
CAMBRIDGESHIRE

What better way to spend a lazy day in the Cambridge sun than punting on the scenic River Cam. Here the New Bridge, also known as the Bridge of Sighs, links the Third Court and New Court of St John's College. The bridge was built in 1831 by Henry Hutchinson and follows the style of the sixteenth-century Bridge of Sighs in Venice. The Venetian bridge housed prisoners, but here the barred windows are to prevent students getting in during the night, not prisoners getting out!

King's College Chapel
CAMBRIDGESHIRE

Uplifting and inspiring, King's College Chapel is perhaps the best example of perpendicular architecture in Britain. The magnificent, soaring stone roof with fan tracery cannot fail to make an impact on all who see it; the sheer scale of human endeavour involved in building this was enormous. The chapel was begun by Henry VI in 1446, but work stopped during the Wars of the Roses, and it was not finally finished until 1515. Among other treasures, the chapel houses *The Adoration of The Magi* by Paul Rubens.

Cavendish
Village Green

SUFFOLK

Time slows down in Suffolk; the air is fresh, the scenery glorious and the traditional English villages are at their most lovely. Pretty houses nestle round the billiard-table green, the church of St Mary casting her benign shadow. The small village of Cavendish is one of many similar treasures to be found in Suffolk. Setting off on a rural road, one comes across any number of 'secret' villages, at the heart of which there is almost always a village green, and generally a good pub!

Southwold

SUFFOLK

This small town sits on a cliff above the North Sea; the lighthouse and the church tower soar into the sky, both beacons of guidance and direction. The lighthouse was built in the 1880s; the church of St Edmund King and Martyr 400 years earlier. Southwold is a charming place, from her picturesque streets to the immaculate village greens. The brightly painted beach huts and attractive beaches make Southwold one of the most popular coastal resorts, but the town still retains much of its original, traditional character.

South-East England

THE COUNTIES OF THE SOUTH-EAST COVER A VAST CORNER OF ENGLAND, FROM THE LIVELY EASTERN COASTLINE OF ESSEX, INLAND TO THE CHALKY CHILTERN HILLS OF BUCKINGHAMSHIRE AND THE WINDBLOWN BERKSHIRE DOWNS, AND SOUTH TO THE FANTASTIC CLIFFS AND BEACHES OF HAMPSHIRE, SUSSEX AND KENT.

Autumn sees the dense beech trees of Buckinghamshire afire with gold and russet red, the Thames snaking through the landscape and into Berkshire, home to Windsor Castle and the magnificent Vale of the White Horse. To the south lies Hampshire with her seafaring traditions, and to the east is Surrey in her manicured perfection. The elegant Surrey homes give way to the grandiose splendour of Sussex, her rolling South Downs – land of sheep and the skylark – leading to the high chalk cliffs of the south coast. Kent, the garden county, sits on the south-east tip of England, and boasts one of the most fertile and productive stretches of farmland. Famous for her fruit-growing and cultivation of hops, Kent's landscape is punctuated by unique, conical oast houses.

The enchanting countryside is just part of the appeal of the South-East, for this is also an area full of delightful villages and bustling, historic towns.

Ivinghoe Beacon
BUCKINGHAMSHIRE

It is hard to believe the Chiltern Hills lie just a few miles north-west of London; their breathtaking beauty, green, rolling hills, valleys, beech woods and wildlife are a nature lover's paradise. The great Ivinghoe Beacon is majestic in the background here. This late Bronze-Age fort sits on one of the highest hills in the Chilterns, and has commanding views across the countryside. It is the oldest such fort, and sits at the head of the Icknield Way, a Roman thoroughfare stretching to East Anglia.

Grand Union Canal
BUCKINGHAMSHIRE

Prior to the massive development of road transport during the 1950s, Britain's canals were vital to its industrial evolution. The Grand Junction Canal, later called the Grand Union Canal in the 1930s, was the main link between London and the rest of the British canal system, the canals forming a web of watery thoroughfares from one end of the country to the other. Today the canals are primarily used for pleasure; the appeal of gliding gently in a long boat has become part of the fabric of Britain's tourist trade.

Medmenham Abbey
BUCKINGHAMSHIRE

The picturesque tranquillity of this scene is far-removed from the lively, exotic and colourful past that this area has known. The original abbey was home to Cistercian monks, known for their frugal and penitent life. By the eighteenth century, the abbey was privately owned and had become the meeting place for the Hell Fire Club – a high-class brothel and the scene of lascivious goings-on. Shielded from the road, the abbey sat above a series of underground caves: the perfect location for undisturbed bad behaviour!

Knebworth House
HERTFORDSHIRE

Opulent and splendid, Knebworth House is a visual delight and never more so than on a summer day when the gardens are in full bloom. The house was begun in 1492 by Sir Robert Lytton, and has remained in the Lytton family ever since. In 1812 part of the building was destroyed, although the grand Tudor Hall survived. In 1843 the first Lord Lytton stamped the exterior with the Gothic style; today the house is a riot of Gothic excess, from its turrets to its gargoyles.

Ashridge Forest
HERTFORDSHIRE

The ancient Ashridge Forest glows with colour, the vibrant oranges and yellows of autumn; a final burst of natural wonder before the onset of winter. This magnificent forest surrounds Ashridge House, a Gothic mansion built by James Wyatt in 1808, with grounds laid out by Capability Brown. The estate extends for six square miles (16 square km) and to the north leads towards Ivinghoe Beacon. The forest is a continuing circle of life, the ancient trees caught in a slow dance from autumn to spring, and spring to autumn.

Belchamp Walter Village Pond
ESSEX

There is something indefinably British about the small village surrounding a green or a pond, and Belchamp Walter is no exception. Here the quiet life of rural Britain revolves around the smooth, flat pond, the quaint, painted houses reflected in the surface. The village pond holds a traditional place in village history, over the centuries being the scene of gatherings, witch-duckings and more. Belchamp Walter's pond is particularly pretty, especially in the summer when the flowers around the banks are in full bloom.

River Stour

ESSEX

The rural delight of such a scene was the inspiration for John Constable, the famous British landscape painter of the early nineteenth century. He was born not far from this spot and grew up along the banks of the River Stour, a landscape of enchantment that remained with him his whole life. The River Stour formed the natural boundary between the kingdoms of Essex and East Anglia in Anglo-Saxon times; now, however, it joins the two counties together through a series of charming bridges.

Canterbury Cathedral

KENT

The fifteenth-century bell tower dominates the skyline of Canterbury. It is particularly poignant at sunset when the dying sun bathes the building in blood-red light, bringing to mind the fate of Thomas Becket, murdered in the cathedral in 1170. This most holy of places is central to Anglican Christianity in Britain and has one of the oldest histories as a site of Christian worship. For centuries it has been a place of pilgrimage; 'The Pilgrim's Way' is a pre-Roman path linking Winchester to Canterbury.

Balloon Festival

KENT

The smooth green fields and brilliant blue sky are a perfect backdrop to the bright hot-air balloons as they take off in a riot of colour – brilliant, boiled-sweet hues lifting up and away. What better way to appreciate the beauty of the countryside fully than with a bird's-eye view? Be prepared for an early start though – the best balloon flights catch the early morning hours, as the landscape starts to come to life in preparation for a new day.

Leeds Castle

KENT

Rising majestically from the still waters of its surrounding moat, Leeds Castle glistens in the soft light, appearing unworldly, the fabric of legend and fantasy. Its history, however, is resoundingly real; the castle has been host to a procession of notable occupants from Catherine of Aragon to Elizabeth I. Leeds is sometimes referred to as the most beautiful of British castles, and it is not hard to see why. Enclosed by 500 acres (202 hectares) of stunning parkland and manicured gardens, this is certainly one of Britain's jewels.

White Cliffs of Dover

KENT

Rising imposingly from the sea, the white cliffs of Dover are as memorable and startling as any natural formation. This dramatic landscape feature, where the rolling North Downs fall into the sea in a tumble of brilliant white chalk, stares across the English Channel towards France. Just 21 miles (34 km) away is Calais and the French coastline. Over the centuries the cliffs have been in the frontline of defence, the first port of call for attacking invaders, but today they remain inextricably bound in a sense of nostalgia.

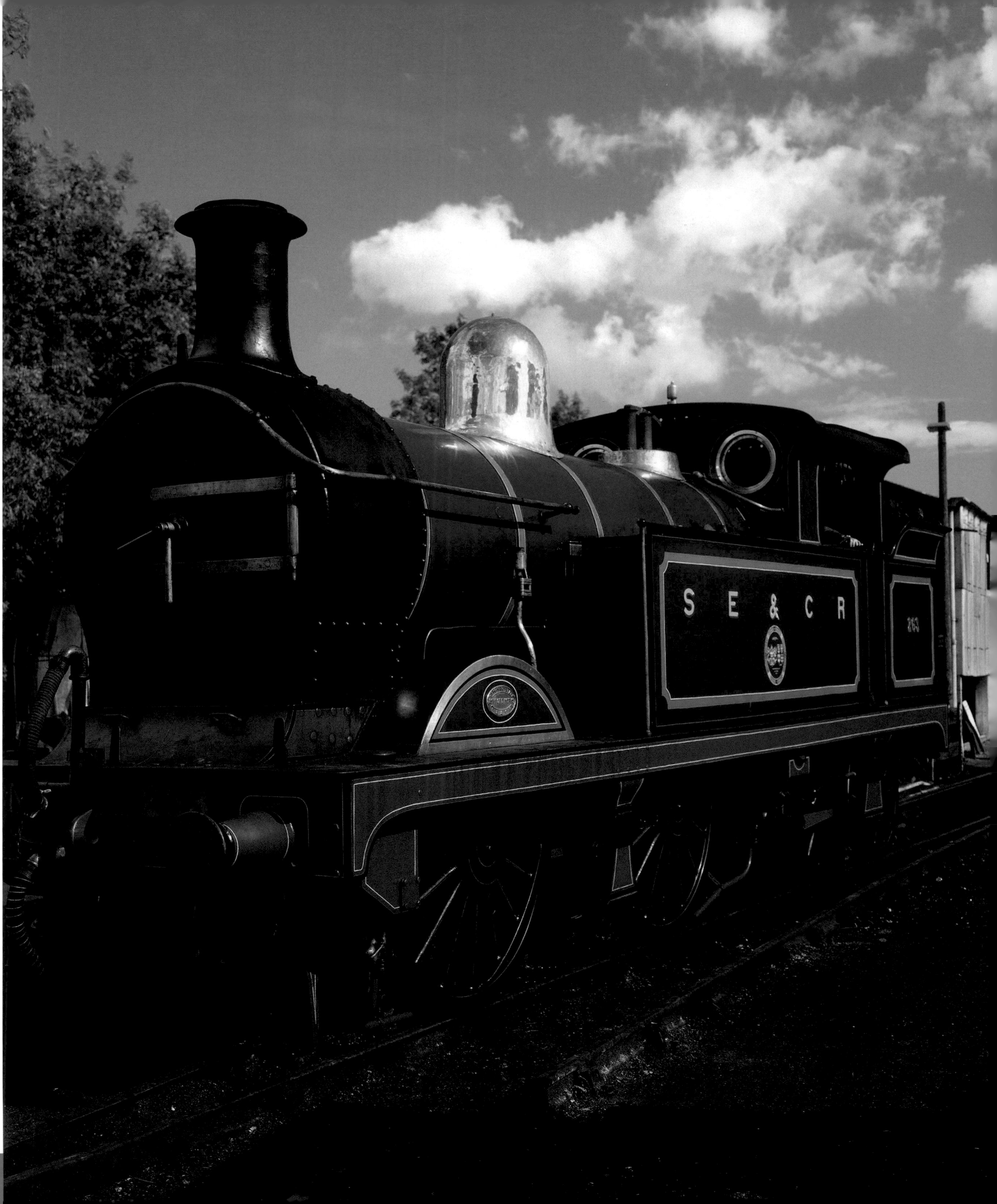
S E & C R

Bluebell Line

SUSSEX

This shiny Type H engine, no. 263, looks every bit as impressive now as it did when it was first commissioned; a relic of the golden age of steam, when Britain's industries and tourism expanded rapidly, due in large part to improved rail transport. The Bluebell Line was Britain's first preserved, standard-gauge passenger railway and re-opened part of the old London to Brighton and South Coast Railway back in 1960. The trains, carriages and wagons are beautifully preserved and continue to operate on a daily basis.

Beachy Head

SUSSEX

Towering 295 feet (90 m) above the sea, Beachy Head is the highest cliff top on the south-east coast of Britain. It is a dramatic spot, the sea crashing below and sea gulls wheeling above, their screams piercing and far-reaching. The original lighthouse was built on the cliff top and was used until 1899, when it threatened to collapse. The new lighthouse was constructed in 1902 by Sir Thomas Matthews, and sits 541 feet (165 m) seawards from the base of the cliffs.

Brighton Royal Pavilion

SUSSEX

The Oriental vision of the Royal Pavilion is one of extravagance, opulence and exuberance – it is one of the most unusual and original buildings in Britain. The building was commissioned by George IV and started out in 1783 as a classical house with a Chinese interior. In 1812 John Nash was engaged to overhaul the building, giving it added flair and whimsy. The Pavilion was at the centre of a divided criticism at the time, and has been subjected to equal measures of derision, intrigue and adoration ever since.

Hastings
SUSSEX

As an island Britain has for a long time had a reputation as a country of fish – the famous English dish of fish and chips is now a worldwide fare; however, it never seems as good as when it has been caught and cooked in Britain. Fishing as an industry has suffered recently, but here the brightly coloured fishing boats line the beach, waiting to go to work. Hastings is home to 'The Stade', a fisherman's beach which boasts the largest fishing fleet worked from the beach in the country.

Hampton Court Palace
SURREY

The magnificent palace was built in 1514 by Cardinal Wolsey and became the favourite country retreat for Henry VIII. It was the scene of court life to the excess, and of 500 years of turbulent history. The grounds still echo with the thunder of horses charging in jousting matches, the roar of the crowds and the melancholy sigh of five of Henry's six wives who lived here. During William III's accession in the seventeenth century, Sir Christopher Wren created the Baroque style of the east front.

Winkworth Arboretum

SURREY

The azure carpet of bluebells is a glorious vibrant strip of lapis lazuli, nature at her best and most vivid. The colour in early summer at the Winkworth Arboretum is rivalled only by the ruby russet of Winkworth's many trees in the autumn. This extraordinary 95-acre (38-hectare) patch of sheer loveliness occupies an area of hillside near to the town of Godalming. Owned by the National Trust since 1952, Winkworth is home to an amazing array of trees, exotic and wild plants, lakes and wildlife.

Crown Inn

SURREY

Overlooking the southern end of Chiddingfold village green is the picturesque medieval timber-framed Crown Inn. Many a beer has been supped here and, according to legend, Elizabeth I 'quenched her thirst herein'. Edward VI also visited the Crown Inn in 1552, giving this historic watering hole a very royal patronage. The beautiful, half-timbered frame of the Crown was only rediscovered during restoration work in 1951. Previously the timbers were hidden by tiles hung in the late-seventeenth century, which accounts for the very fine condition of the beams.

Winchester Cathedral

HAMPSHIRE

Along with Canterbury, Winchester has been the other major place of pilgrimage for Christians in Britain through the ages. The great Winchester Cathedral, which is the longest in Europe, was begun in 1079 and was built in stages over several hundred years. The massive monument to the indomitable spirit of religion presides over the city that was once the capital of England. There is an air of reassuring permanence to Winchester Cathedral; its vast bulk appears as indestructible and stalwart as the beliefs of its faithful leaders.

Micheldever Cottage

HAMPSHIRE

There is nothing quite like an English country cottage garden, and this profusion of flowers outside a thatched cottage in Micheldever would seem to capture precisely everything that a cottage garden should be. The patchwork of summer colours and unruly explosion of natural exuberance is the perfect companion to the cottage's old-world charm. The ancient town of Micheldever, dating back to the Saxons and mentioned in the Domesday Book, is at the heart of Hampshire, and is yet another of this county's idyllic spots.

New Forest Ponies
HAMPSHIRE

William the Conqueror created the New Forest in 1079 to serve as a royal hunting ground, primarily of deer. The beautiful wilderness is home to many different species of trees and plants, as well as wildlife. It is a unique area of historical importance in Britain, and still retains many of the rural practices laid down by the crown in medieval times. One of the most significant of these is the right of the 'commoners' to graze their ponies, cattle, pigs and donkeys across the New Forest acreage.

Beaulieu Palace
HAMPSHIRE

The daffodils at Beaulieu zing with colour, heralding the start of a new spring and closing the door on winter. The beautiful Palace House at Beaulieu is a fitting backdrop for such lovely flowers. Nestled in the heart of the New Forest, Beaulieu was originally the gatehouse to the Beaulieu Abbey. Little remains of the Abbey, but the monastic origins of the house can still be felt. The house, which was rebuilt in the Gothic style in 1872, sits in stunning grounds that extend down to the Beaulieu River.

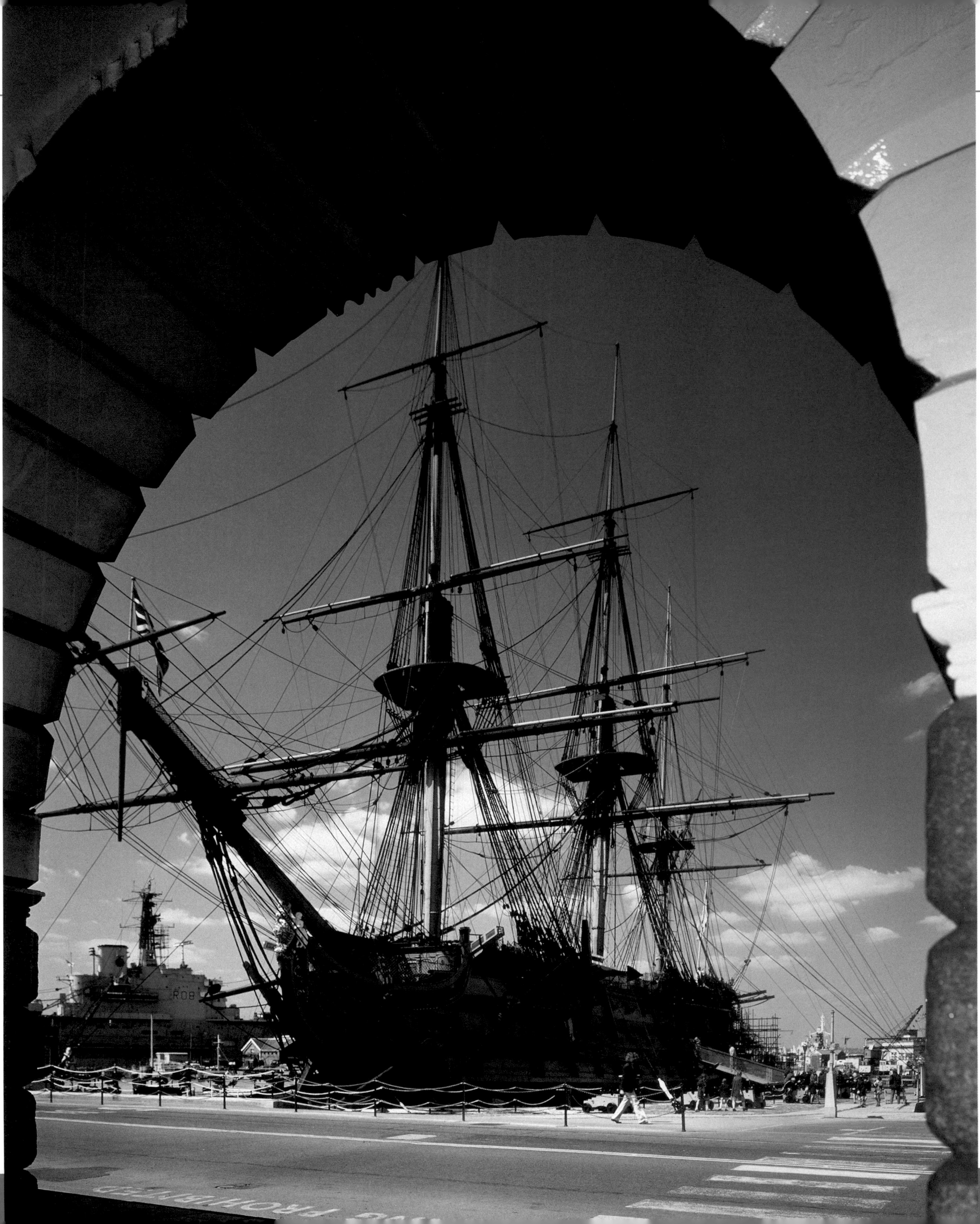

HMS *Victory*

HAMPSHIRE

As majestic now as she was when she rode the high seas, the HMS *Victory* sits resplendent in Portsmouth's Royal Navy Dockyards. She is the world's oldest commissioned warship, and is most famous as being Nelson's flagship during the Battle of Trafalgar. She was retired from active duty in 1812, after 32 years of heroic efforts in the frontline of Britain's navy, and was anchored in Portsmouth harbour for the next 110 years. In 1922 she was moved to a dry dock and carefully restored.

Cowes Week

ISLE OF WIGHT

Sails bowing into the wind, these vibrant boats skim across the smooth surface of the English Channel, competing in the world's most exclusive sailing regatta. The bright sails, set against the surprisingly exotic blue of the Channel, makes this a visual delight. The annual Cowes Week is the Grand National of sailing; a week-long festival of races, parties, shopping, fireworks and more. The event has a historic tradition, having started in 1826, and now sees over 1,000 boats competing.

London

TWO THOUSAND YEARS OF HISTORY ARE CAUGHT UP AMONGST LONDON'S STREETS AND BUILDINGS, THE PAVEMENTS ECHOING WITH THE MEMORY OF HER PAST AND RESOUNDING WITH INTENSITY AS SHE HEADS TOWARDS THE FUTURE.

London is the ultimate melting pot of cosmopolitan life; she is the city that offers everything. Founded around AD 43 by the Romans, the original settlement grew in the area now known as the City's Square Mile. From early beginnings London evolved into a powerhouse, and continues to be the beating heart of Britain's commerce and industry, retail, tourism and entertainment. Growing organically around the River Thames, London is full of surprising, twisting streets, tiny rows of mews houses and urban vistas. Each step brings a new view: a church by Sir Christopher Wren, a square, a park, a statue, a modern glittering office building, a gently sweeping crescent of elegant Regency houses. The capital is home to some of the greatest art galleries, museums, shops and theatres in the world. It is a city of contrasts, from the stately Houses of Parliament to the raucous Leicester Square, the energy of Covent Garden with her market stalls and street performers to the tranquillity of a stroll through Hyde Park.

London Eye and Big Ben

Big Ben and Houses of Parliament

Framed in a night sky of glowing red, Big Ben appears within the great London Eye, a juxtaposition of old and new, each as aesthetically pleasing as the other. This beautiful sunset view blocks out the noise and bustle of London, leaving only a landscape of infinite calm. The London Eye, created as a millennium landmark, slowly revolves and offers visitors views of up to 25 miles (40 km) across some of London's greatest buildings, and as far as Windsor Castle in the distance.

The stately Gothic grace of the Houses of Parliament was created between 1840 and 1860 by Sir Charles Barry and A.W. Pugin, who built this 'new' building on the site of the former royal residence; this is one of the most universally recognised buildings in Britain. Jostled up to the Houses of Parliament stands Big Ben, the statuesque clock tower that rings melodically across London. Big Ben is actually the name of the largest bell in the tower, which was cast in 1858.

Trooping the Colour, Horse Guards

Trafalgar Square

Lined up in bright rows of ruby red, the troops from the Household Division take part in the traditional Trooping the Colour, a ceremony that marks the Queen's official birthday. This ceremony has been used to honour the sovereign's birthday since 1748, and is just one of many richly historic traditions for which Britain is famous. The event is held on Horse Guards Parade, Whitehall; during Trooping the Colour the Queen is given a royal salute and she inspects the troops before they march past her.

The towering Norwegian Spruce Christmas tree is a beacon of fairy lights, lending a magical feel to an already magical place – Trafalgar Square at night in the run up to Christmas. The tree has been donated every year since 1947 by the city of Oslo in Norway to the City of Westminster, as a token of appreciation for Britain's friendship during the Second World War. Seen here, the towering tree reflects the steeple of St Martin-in-the-Fields, both graceful and beautifully lit.

Buckingham Palace

A horizontal sweep of classical grandeur set behind a slash of red and yellow – spring is perhaps the best time of year to see this stately palace. Buckingham Palace has been the main royal residence since Queen Victoria moved here in 1837. Prior to that, the palace had relatively humble beginnings, originally being a town house for the Duke of Buckingham. John Nash created the palace in 1820 and it was later remodelled by Edward Blore. The Classical façade was added in 1913 by Sir Aston Webb.

St James's Park

Such a peaceful scene could be deep in the heart of the country, but instead it is St James's Park, another of London's oases of green and tranquillity. This is one of the oldest of London's parks, and also one of the smallest. It has a very royal location, sitting as it does between three palaces: Buckingham Palace, St James's Palace, and Westminster. The park dates back to the thirteenth century, but it was Charles II who formally landscaped the space and opened it to the public.

Regent Street Christmas Lights

The Christmas lights hover, suspended above Regent Street; magical, exciting and fantastic, they inspire a little of the Christmas spirit in all but the most miserable of souls. The lights were first introduced in 1954 when an article in the *Daily Telegraph* commented on how dull London looked. They were lit every year until 1971, when the tradition was stopped for economic reasons. It was reinstated in 1978, and they have been lighting up Christmas ever since, famously turned on by a celebrity of the moment.

Somerset House

Somerset House gives the term 'office building' a whole new meaning, and yet that is specifically what it was designed for during the eighteenth century. The first building of its kind in England, it was built to house important government offices and the Royal Academy of Arts. It was in fact designed by one of the founder members of the Royal Academy, Sir William Chambers, between 1776 and 1786. Somerset House sits on the site of an older house, built in 1547 for Edward Seymour, Duke of Somerset.

City of London from Waterloo Bridge

St Paul's Cathedral

One of the most stunning visual aspects to London is the combination of old and new buildings; the coupling of modern skyscrapers with historic churches, the one a temple to commerce, the other to religion. The skyline of the city is a case in point. The dome of St Paul's Cathedral, built by Sir Christopher Wren, sits resplendent amongst shining towers of glass and steel. The view from Waterloo Bridge provides one of the most captivating vistas of the City of London, especially on a fine, sunny day.

The open-top bus tour is one of the capital's best-loved tourist attractions, and here the bus passes one of the most significant of London sights. The City of London has been watched over by a St Paul's Cathedral since AD 604; the current one was built between 1675 and 1710 by Sir Christopher Wren, following the destruction of the previous cathedral during the Great Fire of London. St Paul's is the scene of most major commemorative events in the country, from coronations to funerals and remembrance services.

City of London from Tower Bridge

In the heart of London lies the City, one square mile (2.6 square km) and domicile to the nation's high finance. The buildings are the same eclectic mix of old and new that London is so famous for, although the modern skyscrapers now dominate the skyline. This is where London began; the site of the original Londinium built within the second-century Roman walls. The Tower of London, grand in the distance and the scene of much bloodshed, looks towards the elegant 'Gherkin', a stunning feat of modern engineering.

Tower of London

This fortress has a history stretching back to William the Conqueror who built the great White Tower in around 1097. During the thirteenth century the White Tower was fortified with two lines of defensive walls and the Royal Mint was moved there, safe behind the thick walls. The Tower was used as a palace, fortress and prison, holding captive such royals as Anne Boleyn, Lady Jane Grey and the Duke of Monmouth, before they were executed in the centre of the complex on Tower Green.

Millennium Dome

The ethereal glow of the Millennium Dome by night lends the structure an unearthly, phantasmagoric appeal. Quite unlike anything else built before, the Dome appears to hover above the ground, caught in a transitory place – a quality that in part reflects the chequered history and future of this huge structure. Unveiled for the millennium, the Dome failed to attract the crowds, cost millions of pounds, and closed one year later. Now talk of creating a sports arena and entertainment centre beneath her ghostly walls suggests a step forward for the building.

Thames Flood Barrier

One could be forgiven for mistaking the Thames Flood Barrier for a piece of modern sculptural art; great shining steel pods rearing up from the water like a series of impressive sentries. The flood barrier is actually an extraordinary piece of engineering, a system of vast steel gates that can be raised in the event of an emergency. Continual threat of flooding along the Thames Estuary expedited the building of the flood barrier, and it was finally unveiled in 1982 by Queen Elizabeth II.

South-West England

From the rugged, untamed coastlines of Cornwall and Devon to the enigmatic Salisbury Plain in Wiltshire, the unsurpassable elegance of the historic town of Bath in Avon to the towering cliffs and gorges of the Mendip Hills in Somerset and the wild heathlands of Thomas Hardy country in Dorset; the South-West of England holds an infinite and indefinable appeal.

It is an area inextricably bound with legend and mystery, the shadow of King Arthur and his knights woven into the very fabric of Cornish life and landscape. The romantically picturesque moorlands of Devon, characterised by Dartmoor's desolate beauty, are stage indeed for great plays of the imagination. Neighbouring Somerset is rich in lush green pastures, a county of farmers and fishermen; in nearby Avon is the ancient town of Bath. Across Dorset, chalk hills undulate gently, rolling into the huge chalk cliffs stretching from Lyme Regis to Burton Bradstock. Small and lovely villages typify Dorset's rural charm, scattered amongst large tracts of productive dairy farmland that cross into Wiltshire.

Yet again a rich tapestry of contrasts, the South-West remains breathtakingly beautiful and largely unspoilt; mysterious, wild, charming and exhilarating, the South-West of England is a destination to inspire all the senses.

Stonehenge

WILTSHIRE

Wide-open Salisbury Plain exudes a sense of mystery; the presence of an ancient history is tangible here, alive still, but not understood. Stonehenge sits at the heart of the plain – silent, brooding stones, monuments to something beyond our reach. This is the best preserved of the Bronze-Age sites, a structure built over thousands of years, with an almost incomprehensible effort of sheer manpower and dedication. This ancient temple continues to inspire all those who see it, moved by the inexplicable sense of part elation, part fear.

Salisbury Cathedral

WILTSHIRE

The magnificent early English Gothic building of Salisbury Cathedral is one of the finest surviving examples of this type of architecture. The soaring verticality of the building and fine sculptural work cannot fail to uplift a weary soul. The cathedral is unique because it was conceived and built as a single unit, unlike almost every other building of this size. Work began in 1220 and the cathedral was completed in an extraordinarily fast 60 years. Only the spire, the tallest in England, was added separately in 1334.

Longleat House

WILTSHIRE

Longleat House was started in 1568 by Sir John Thynne and is a fine example of an early Renaissance home. The stately building is set in 900 acres (364 hectares) of grounds, the gardens of which were laid out by the famous landscaper Capability Brown. The house is as famous for its ornate ceilings and abundant use of gilt as it is for its eccentric owner, the 7th Marquess of Bath. Longleat also houses a particularly impressive library, which is home to the 'First Folio' of William Shakespeare's plays.

Clifton Suspension Bridge

AVON

Soaring across the spectacular Avon Gorge in Bristol is the Clifton Suspension Bridge, itself almost as dramatic as the limestone cliffs that it joins. The bridge was begun in 1831, built to the designs of Isambard Kingdom Brunel – amazingly it was his first major commission. The project suffered from financial and political hindrances and was abandoned, half-built, in 1843. Brunel died unexpectedly, and in 1853 work resumed on the bridge – now it was to be his memorial. Today it remains magnificent, modern beyond its time and unremittingly awe-inspiring.

West Doors of Bath Abbey

AVON

The spectacular Bath Abbey sits right at the heart of Bath and on the site of two previous churches. The first dated from AD 757 but was destroyed in 1066; a second Norman church replaced it, but by the end of the fifteenth century this too was in ruins. The present abbey was begun in 1499, and is one of the last great medieval abbeys. The West Front is captivating and has carved angels climbing up and down ladders on each of the turrets flanking the window

Roman Baths
AVON

Seen by night, the Roman Baths in Bath are a haunting place of ethereal beauty, the soft lights reflected in the flat, still surface of a seemingly bottomless pool. These are the best-preserved Roman remains in Britain, and demonstrate just how advanced the Romans were with technology. Adjacent to the baths is the Georgian Pump Room, a lovely, Neoclassical room of great sophistication, where water was drawn for drinking. The baths were central to society in Roman times, and retained their position of importance for centuries.

Royal Crescent
AVON

Across a glorious profusion of colour, the elegant façade of the Royal Crescent is just visible. Bath is one of the finest Georgian towns and retains much of its original character. The Royal Crescent, beautifully positioned against the formal brilliance of Victoria Park, was built to the designs of John Wood the Younger between 1767 and 1774. It is a masterpiece of the best architecture and decoration of the time, and was built to accommodate wealthy visitors to the town. Number One, Royal Crescent is now home to the Bath Preservation Trust.

Pulteney Bridge

AVON

The extraordinary Pulteney Bridge, designed by Robert Adam in 1770, is one of only four bridges in the world to house shops, and clearly shows its debt to the Ponte Vecchio in Florence and Ponte di Rialto in Venice. The bridge was commissioned by the entrepreneurial William Pulteney to join Bath with an area ripe for development on the opposite side of the river. Over the years, the bridge was greatly changed with detrimental effect, but in 1975 it was thoroughly restored and remains one of Bath's greatest treasures.

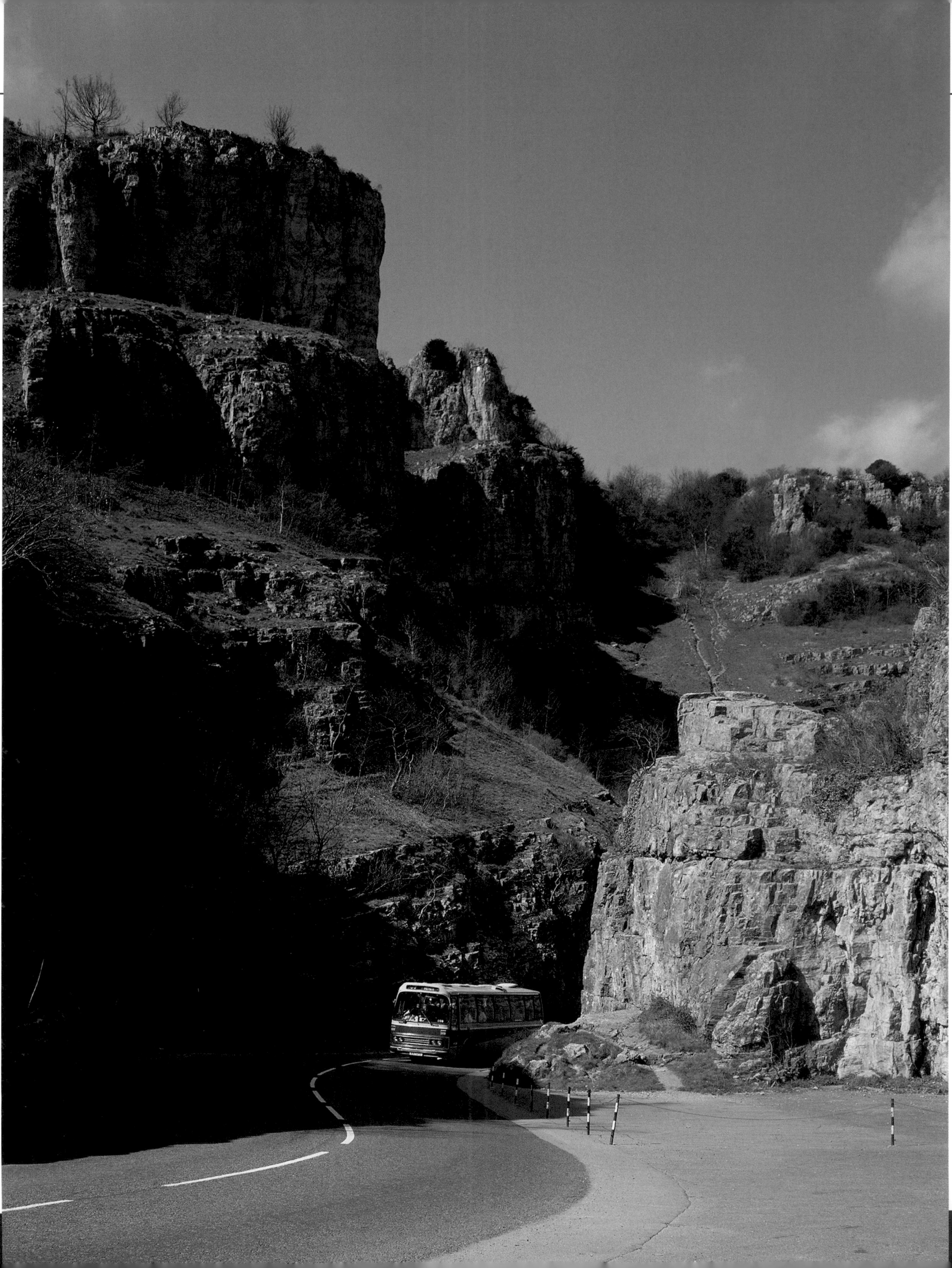

Cheddar Gorge

SOMERSET

Deep in Somerset lies one of the most spectacular natural wonders of Britain, the Cheddar Gorge. Great limestone cliffs soar to an incredible 450 feet (137 m) above sea level, making them the highest cliffs in the country. Once a great river would have cut this swathe through the limestone; now the river runs underground leaving its legacy of cliffs and caves behind. This is an ancient place, the many caves having offered shelter to early man. Now they are home to the rare horseshoe bat and many species of birds.

Wells Cathedral

SOMERSET

Wells grew around the natural springs, deemed to have healing powers, that are now in the grounds of Bishop's Palace. A church was built near the wells in AD 705 and the present cathedral was then built on this site from 1180. Wells Cathedral is one of the most impressive cathedrals in Britain, and the west front with its carved statues is the building's crowning glory. The façade was built between 1209 and 1250, and 300 of the original, over-life-size medieval statues have survived.

Glastonbury Abbey
SOMERSET

Steeped in legend and mystery, Glastonbury Abbey is reputed to be the final resting place of King Arthur and Queen Guinevere; Arthur's spirit still roams the ruins. This is believed to be the site of the earliest Christian church in Britain, and dates back to the seventh century, although the remains are mostly Norman. The abbey became one of the most powerful in the land until Henry VIII hanged the abbot in 1539 and destroyed many of the buildings, using the stone for building elsewhere.

Minehead
SOMERSET

Minehead nestles on the pretty Somerset coastline, sandwiched between the heather-topped moorlands of Exmoor and the Bristol Channel, and sheltered to the north by North Hill. This is the most westerly of Somerset's towns and encompasses a lively 'new town' and the historic older town that sprawls on to the slopes of North Hill. This part, Quay Town, revolves around the harbour, which dates back to 1616. Thatched cottages and narrow streets such as Church Steps are typical of the town's picturesque appeal.

Porlock Bay

SOMERSET

The open spaces of Exmoor tumble down towards Porlock Bay in a blaze of purple and yellow, to join the sea of brilliant blue. On a fine summer's day, with just a puff of wind to chivvy the clouds across the sky, the call of seagulls and a warm sun – this is a scene of astonishing beauty. Behind the bay sits an inland salt marsh, a private paradise for a number of unusual wading birds and wildfowl, and a stop-off for little egrets, spoonbills and marsh harriers as they wheel through.

Shaftesbury

DORSET

Shaftesbury is Dorset's most ancient hilltop town, and sits 700 feet (213 m) on a plateau above the fertile Blackmoor Vale. The view from the town is stunning; this is the productive basin of Dorset, a dairy farming area rich in trees, rivers and beautiful green pastures. Shaftesbury is a pretty settlement, with cobbled streets and green-grey, limestone houses. Gold Hill sweeps down towards the vale; the houses are terraced like an Italian hill town on one side and buttressed on the other.

Durdle Door

DORSET

To the east of Dorset lies Bournemouth and to the west Weymouth, but in between can be found some of the most exciting coastline on the south coast. Here the Chaldon Downs end abruptly in white cliffs, which in turn shelter smooth, sandy beaches that brace the ultramarine blue of the sea on a clear day. Durdle Door is a natural archway of Purbeck limestone that juts out into the sea, forming the eastern end of Durdle Door Cove. The white chalk headland, Bats Head, marks the western point of the cove.

Watermouth Cove

DEVON

Devon's coastline scenes, from the southern point of Welcombe near the Cornish border up to Trentishoe on the north coast, are some of the most wild and ruggedly beautiful to be found in Britain. This is the coast of crashing waves, huge rocks and jutting headlands, so Watermouth Cove forms a peaceful respite. Here the sea is smooth, the beaches shingle and attractive. The nearby small town of Ilfracombe is a popular resort and offers all kinds of boat trips, fishing and golfing for the relaxed holidaymaker.

Combestone Tor

DEVON

The open wilderness of Dartmoor is one of desolate beauty and rough appeal – it offers some of the best horseback riding and hiking in the country, and is home to a wide range of wildlife. Scattered across Dartmoor are a series of tors, impressive rock towers of many layers. One could be forgiven for assuming they are manmade, such is their precisely stacked appearance. Actually they are natural formations, granite rock piles that have been eroded over the centuries by the harsh climate of the open landscape.

Clovelly Harbour

DEVON

The small village of Clovelly sits in a narrow passage of land between two steep cliffs on the site of an ancient settlement. The village is mentioned in the Domesday Book, but was probably first established by the Saxons. This is a quaint fishing village that has more recently benefited from the tourist industry. Part of Clovelly's appeal lies in its beautiful cottages, flowers and working harbour, but it is also only open to pedestrians – all cars are banned – and this makes it a quiet corner of tranquillity.

Bedruthan Steps

CORNWALL

Cornwall – land of sea, sun and fantastic scenery. The coastline is picturesque in its essence; golden, sandy beaches, black headlands, blue seas and wild flowers. It is an area of legend and mystery, the fairytale landscape adding to the unique charm of this most southerly part of Britain. This scene is typical of Cornwall's coastline; the great granite rocks peppered across the bay are the Bedruthan Steps, allegedly created by the giant Bedruthan to traverse from one end of the bay to the other.

Wheal Coates Old Engine House

CORNWALL

Standing stark against the sky, the ruins of the Wheal Coates Engine House at first glance appear religious, abandoned from an ancient site of Christianity. Their history is far less civilized. These buildings, halfway down the cliffs just north of the pretty cove of Chapel Porth, housed the engines used to pump water out of the sunken mine shafts. Tin mining was big business here in the nineteenth century; however, conditions were poor and loss of life was a common occurrence.

Polperro Harbour

CORNWALL

This old fishing village is now a popular destination for holidaymakers, drawn to the pretty, lime-washed houses and slow pace of life. Polperro is everything that a traditional Cornish fishing village typifies: quaint buildings surrounding a small harbour sheltered by two sea walls, narrow cobbled streets and the whispers of smugglers' ghosts echoing through the buildings. Cornwall's coast is famous for the tales of smugglers, their triumphs and their demise, and Polperro is home to her fair share of their stories.

Godrevy Lighthouse

CORNWALL

In the far west of Cornwall is St Ives, a picturesque town of cobbled streets, lovely buildings and sandy beaches. Off the coast of St Ives, situated on a small island, is the Godrevy Lighthouse, standing a lonely watch over the Stones, a treacherous reef stretching for 1½ miles (2.4 km). This was the scene of the devastating shipwreck of the *Nile*, a passenger steamer, in 1854 – all lives were lost. Godrevy was also the inspiration for Virginia Woolf's novel *To The Lighthouse*.

Land's End

CORNWALL

This is the most westerly point of Britain, separated from the Scilly Isles and the coast of America by miles and miles of sea. It is a place of legend, mystery and folklore; the landscape inspiring, evocative and beautiful. Here the great Penwith Peninsular falls into the sea in a mass of rock. The sun sets, one last dying orange flare dropping into the sea and leaving this place of infinite magic, great natural sculptures of granite holding the secrets of times gone by.

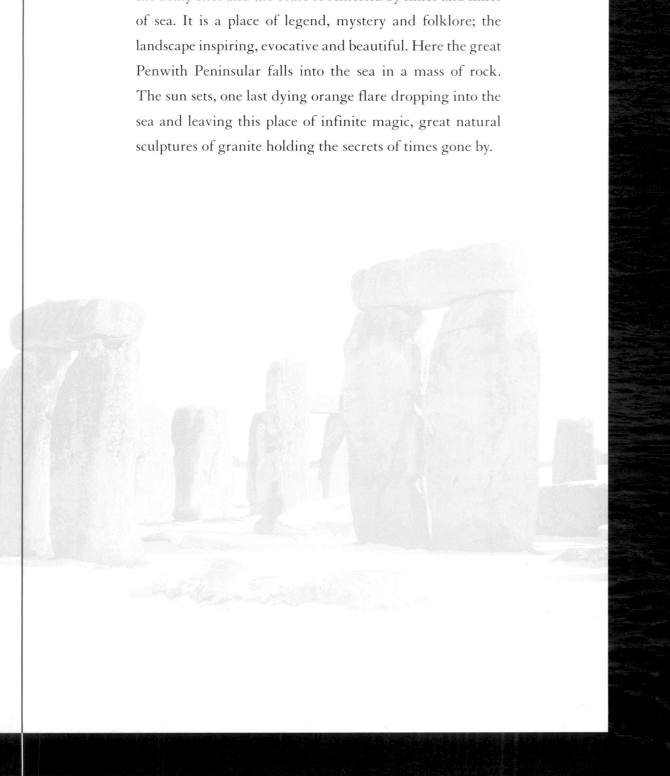

Index